FISCHL

ELIZABETH AVEDON EDITIONS

VINTAGE CONTEMPORARY ARTISTS

VINTAGE BOOKS

A DIVISION OF RANDOM HOUSE NEW YORK

A Vintage Contemporary Artists Original, November 1987
FIRST EDITION

Copyright © 1987 by Elizabeth Avedon

Library of Congress Cataloging-in-Publication Data
Fischl, Eric, 1948–
Eric Fischl.
(Vintage contemporary artists series)
"A Vintage original."
Bibliography: p.
1. Fischl, Eric, 1948–   —Interviews.
2. Artists—United States—Interviews.
3. Art, American.   4. Art,
Modern—20th century—United States.
I. Kuspit, Donald B. (Donald Burton), 1935–
II. Avedon, Elizabeth.   III. Title.   IV. Series.
N6537.F475A35   1987   709'.2'4   86-404667
ISBN 0-394-74789-5 (pbk.)

COVER PHOTOGRAPH © 1987 BY RICHARD AVEDON

BACK COVER: *Portrait of the Artist as an Old Man,* 1984.
Oil/linen; 85″ × 70″. Collection of the
San Francisco Museum of Modern Art, San Francisco.
Courtesy Mary Boone Gallery. Photo: Zindman/Fremont.

Manufactured in the United States of America
10 9 8 7 6 5 4 3 2 1

AN INTERVIEW
WITH
ERIC FISCHL
BY DONALD KUSPIT

INTRODUCTION

Eric Fischl's paintings have been described as "Freudian," but—still psychoanalytically speaking—they are best described in terms of "object relations" theory. They are about the crises of adolescent sexuality, but, more crucially, they are about the emotion we invest in parental and other "objects"—in the adults with authority over us we always carry around within us, and in the things associated with them. Fischl's pictures are about not just desire as such, but desire in the service of freedom from parental tyranny. It is a paradoxical desire, for it not only has the parental figures as its object but represents a rebellion against them. Thus, in *Sleepwalker*, 1979, Fischl's first fully articulated statement of purpose, as it were, the point is not that the boy is masturbating in the wading pool, but that his masturbation is defiant of his parents, unconsciously present in and represented by the empty lawn chairs. Standing in the wading pool, which is symbolic of the infantile state of dependence he wishes to leave behind, he asserts his manhood and autonomy by masturbating. But his parents can be the only objects he has in mind, apart from the self he is vigorously expressing by his ritual act. Fischl's picture, like all the others, is an allegory of ambivalence.

Similarly, in *Dog Days*, 1983, the parental figure leaves the scene, abandoning the two impudent "dogs" to their sexual devices. But the balcony fence remains, symbolic of adult constraint. The sexual message is "don't fence me in"—both the boy and the

3

girl have dropped their pants—but it is not clear that what has begun so hopefully will climax in an adult way. One never sees the orgasmic moment of consummation in a Fischl picture, the adult follow-through of successful sexual relations. One only sees the proposed intimacy—a desire for bodily intimacy that may be more an expression of a need for human closeness in a world in which the adolescent feels isolated than strictly sexual in import. Indeed, the fact that the dogs and adolescents are interchangeable suggests that the sexuality may be a fantasy. Fischl may have given us a version of Chuang-tzu's dream of himself as a butterfly, and of his uncertainty whether he was a man dreaming of being a butterfly, or a butterfly dreaming of being a man. Do we have well-behaved —when their adult owner is present—little dogs dreaming of being wild adolescents breaking the rules of propriety, or adolescents thinking of breaking the rules of civilized relationships and self-protectively dreaming of becoming good little pets? Do we read the diptych from left to right or right to left?

In *Birthday Boy*, 1982, *Slumber Party*, 1983, and the right panel of *A Visit to/A Visit from the Island*, 1983, it is not clear that sexual consummation is truly in the offing. One has, rather, the littleness of the boy in the presence of the looming, almost gigantic— certainly awesome—female, a juxtaposition emphasizing the boy's melancholy feeling of inadequacy. It is not even clear that the sexual relationship is implied by the nakedness of the figures, which seems more casually social—a way of being outspokenly

4

informal—than invitingly carnal. It is all in the spectator's own ambivalent wishes.

Are Fischl's pictures pornographic? One need only pick up a pornographic magazine, whether soft-core or hard-core, to see that they are not. His figures are far from alluring, and their sexual organs are not particularly featured, however subliminally sexual their relationship may be. Their nakedness is not so much sexually as emotionally provocative, for it confirms the loneliness of the figures. It is more of a psychological than a physical nakedness. Fischl has said that he is concerned with grasping the pathos of youth as it gropes toward self-awareness. He has said that our society offers no aid to youth in this process. In Fischl, sexuality is more the vehicle of lonely self-discovery and self-projection than an end in itself. His pictures are really about the vulnerability of youth rather than its sexual interests and explorations. His pictures are about the existential quandary inherent in every intensely significant human relationship. It remains problematic until its participants work their way through the master/slave paradigm of the adult/child relationships on which all relationships are initially modeled. This is the only way their relationships can endure and mature—be successful. But unconsciously they are likely to get bogged down in the archaic pattern. In a sense, Fischl depicts the stalemate of the adult/child relationship. There are no really successful relationships in his pictures, although all are full of the profound hidden significance of that first relationship. The peculiar dissociation of the figures, for all their apparent related-ness, suggests this double meaning.

Fischl's realism has a photographic basis, but he uses "unreal-istic" painterliness and almost manneristically complex compo-sition, both with a virtuoso sense of control, to create an unconscious—uncanny—meaning that an ordinary photographic surface cannot communicate. His art's brilliance is that while it remains true to the American Scene it is aesthetically sophisticated beyond anything the American social realists were capable of. And it is more pessimistic than such realism ever thought of becoming. Fischl's realism may be connected, as has often been said, to the realism of Edward Hopper—the tradition of the isolated figure (not entirely bleak; it is too full of itself for that) that reaches back to Winslow Homer and Thomas Eakins—but Fischl has assimilated and put to special use two major techniques of modernism—radical gesturalism and collage fragmentation—that were beyond the so-cial realists. His touch scoops out the everyday objective surface of his picture to imply its latent subjective content, and his scenes are indirectly collage compositions, the figures and backgrounds pieced together from different sources. The fragmentary sense of composition remains an undertow adding its unconscious import to the event depicted.

Fischl's work is part of the new narrative art that has emerged in the eighties. What makes his narrative method distinctive is that each picture hints at a core story that is never quite completely told. The story seems well known, but isn't. It seems obvious, but there's something disturbingly enigmatic about it. It has been said that the task of art today is to maintain mystery in a world that thinks there is none. In this age of overexposure art becomes a subtle way of underexposing, not to artificially generate a sense of mystery, but to remind us that there are experiences that are incompletely analyzable but have profound effect. It is exactly with these fundamental life experiences that Fischl's art deals. Fischl seems to be showing all, but what counts in his work is what is not stated, and can never be adequately stated. Fischl's pictures seem to promise us clarity about complex issues, but in fact suggest depth of a complexity that can never be fully deciphered. It is this that makes his pictures peculiarly opaque dreams, abysses of meaning we can never quite climb out of once we have accepted their terms.

Under the veneer of dealing with the affluent society and its neuroses—he has acknowledged that he is dealing with the failings of suburban life, with its pretense to mythical happiness—Fischl narrates a struggle between Eros and Thanatos. His pictorial veneer is incisively shaped and finely polished, but there is a strange murkiness behind it, echoed particularly in the vehement touch, at once quirky and titillating. There has been much talk about the erotic character of Fischl's scenes, but death is also strongly present, whether overt or covert. There are scenes with drowned figures, and with figures that look as if the boat they're in might capsize at any moment. There is a powerful aggression, a lurking violence, in many of the works. To understand its full import, one has only to recall Freud's idea, in his late thought, that aggression is one's own death instinct directed toward others. The scene could as easily turn into one of conflict as one of love. I see more aggression than sexuality—more of a desire to destroy the other than to unite with him or her—in the supposedly erotic scenes. The separateness of the figures seems fraught with impacted tension, even emotional violence. There is more frustration than satisfaction. The figures not only hardly bond, but the very thought of bonding seems like bondage to them. Refusal of this bondage may explain their peculiar inertia and nonrelatedness. Indeed, the very indefiniteness of the scenes—the frequent difficulty in determining what is occurring—does a certain violence to them. It also administers a violent slap to the spectator's face, as if to destroy his or her distance from the scenes. Like a movie, Fischl's pictures seem to warn us: "You may not know it, but this is your life, so you'd better watch out."

One can no doubt overpsychologize about Fischl's works, but many of them, especially the group scenes, are clearly fantasies. Fischl does not simply inhabit a traditional style, as is the postmodernist wont, but puts it to "fantastic" use to generate a new sense of content—of the import of content for any style. In a world that has become addicted to "style," whatever that style may be, Fischl, by making a familiar style subtly strange, points to the power of content. Content is presented as powerful in itself, and as disruptive of habitual horizons of expectation. He shows us that an authentic content forces us to identify with it against our will; it overcomes our resistance to it and forces its inevitability upon us. His work is not only semantically and syntactically subtle—creative by making many subtle changes in the semantics and syntax of a conveniently representational imagery—but "pragmatically" subtle in that it theatrically engages us. His pictures are stage sets on which we can act out the fiction of our most hidden selves. Fischl's art is truly a therapeutic regression, accomplished by a subtle manipulation of the repressed eager to make its return. His works insinuate themselves into us through the fact that at first glance they seem to be conceived in everyday terms, and as such harmlessly perceived, for all the bizarreness of their scenes. But once inside us, they tear the scabs off our sense of the tragic. Fischl shows that that sense still festers beneath our somnambulist complacency. Unexpectedly, the tragic point of view is the child's point of view, which Fischl deliberately takes. Fischl shows the world as the vulnerable child sees it, but he suggests that we can achieve adulthood—ego strength—by accepting the tragic character of the child. He reminds us of our doubly tragic lives: once tragic children, we become tragic adults by accepting the fact that our childhood was tragic. Contemporary America is unaccustomed to such elementary tragic truth, such primal knowledge.

COLOR PLATES

IMITATING THE DOG (MOTHER AND DAUGHTER II), 1984.
Oil/canvas; 96″ × 84″.
Collection of Hugh and Lee Freund, New York.
Courtesy Mary Boone Gallery.
Photo: Zindman/Fremont.

A BRIEF HISTORY OF NORTH AFRICA, 1985.
Oil/linen; 88″ × 120″.
Private collection, New York.
Courtesy Mary Boone Gallery.
Photo: Zindman/Fremont.

VANITY, 1984.
Oil/canvas; 108″ × 96″.
Collection of Michael and Judy Ovitz, Los Angeles.
Courtesy Mary Boone Gallery.
Photo: Zindman/Fremont.

THE INTERVIEW

DK: *Let's start with some simple facts about your life. When and where were you born?*

EF: I was born in 1948 in New York City.

DK: *Did you grow up in New York?*

EF: No. When I was an infant, my family moved to Long Island, where I lived until I was eighteen.

DK: *What town did you live in?*

EF: Port Washington. It's a suburban, commuter town.

DK: *Did your family have its own house or did you live in an apartment?*

EF: We had a house. We actually moved several times in those eighteen years. We had several houses.

DK: *All in suburban Port Washington?*

EF: Yes.

DK: *Did any of these houses have a swimming pool?*

EF: No, we belonged to a yacht club.

DK: *I'm asking you about the facts of your life in suburbia because I think it's important to know them to understand your pictures of suburban life. Do you agree?*

EF: I'm not sure. As a child it was just a great amount of fun to belong to the yacht club. It was something to look forward to.

DK: Some critics have suggested that your mother's alcoholism is directly connected to some of your images. Can it be said in general that your attitude to your mother and father is indirectly reflected in your art?

EF: Well, when you're a child growing up in paradise, there's no such thing as a fact of life. You don't make any separation between the things that are promised you and reality. Everything that is promised is supposed to be delivered, but when it isn't—when you have a tragedy like a debilitated or invalid parent—it shapes the very foundations of everything you do. The tragic fact doesn't correspond with the visual experience of suburban paradise. It doesn't correspond with the things that you're surrounded with, which are supposed to symbolize your life and also to insulate it.

I once had an experience in Arizona, where my father lives in a new area of Phoenix. It's quite an extraordinary place because it's an architectural fantasy. It's a condominium complex based on pseudo-Mediterranean architecture. So it's like when you're there, you're not there, right? There's also this thing in the Southwest called desert planting, where they organize the desert into microcosms, small perfect microcosms.

I was walking through his neighborhood and I was feeling depressed. I was very introspective, melancholy. I'm not sure how to name the mood, but it wasn't pleasant. I was feeling out of sorts. And as I was walking through the neighborhood I was looking at this scene of incredible tranquility, this incredible illusion of tranquility. It was visually in front of me, but I wasn't attuned to it. The incredible order of these desert planted gardens struck me. They were perfectly ordered, unlike my feelings. The houses were silent and there was this wonderful lushness to the area. It was bizarre to see that lushness in the desert. The discrepancy, the contradiction between my bad mood and the gorgeous surroundings hit me.

DK: When did you have this experience?

EF: Eight to ten years ago—something like that. I realized that what I had going inside me was out of kilter with what I was seeing. My feelings didn't match up to what I think of as a visual projection of how you should feel and how you should order life. So I felt completely displaced. I remember that this was how I felt as a child. This was what I felt like in the suburbs. I have always felt very alienated from the suburbs precisely because of the turmoil of my emotions.

There is one other point that I want to make. The suburbs are based on visual presentation, visual stimulation. I think that the reason I'm a painter has everything to do with this fact. It doesn't surprise me that I became a painter rather than a sculptor or a musician or something like that. It's simply because the suburbs always try to represent themselves to themselves through a look. Everyone tried to live up to the image of the kind of ideal life promised by the look of the suburban scene and invested all their feelings in that effort. And when life wasn't so ideal, the feelings suffered all the more because of the investment in the look, the ideal living implied by the scene. It's a common suburban experience to go into a house where the kitchen looks just like a magazine photograph that represents the ideal kitchen. It's a very direct equation.

DK: Would it be fair to say that what fascinates you about the suburbs is that they project a kind of stage set for happiness, a highly artificial world in which the image of what ideal life is supposed to be according to our society has become fact? As you said, the dream kitchen existed in reality. Yet the people inhabiting the American version of the perfect place were far from happy. They really didn't even have it within reach. The suburbs are a kind of harmonious place, but the harmony is a fiction, a masquerade. The outward look mocks one's feelings.

EF: That's right. The harmony is purely visual. And, of course, experience taught one that suburban life was quite the opposite of the way it looked. The reality is that it is filled with what life is usually filled with, which is turmoil.

DK: *In looking at your pictures, I've always had the sense that the world you present is strangely grotesque in its artificiality and that people who inhabit it are in another mental world. They don't fit into the look, even though they live in the suburbs. It's almost as though they've dropped in from another planet. Is that a fair statement? I recall one picture in which an adolescent boy watches television almost addictively. The television set has a primitive tribal sculpture on it, which seems to signal the boy's primitive emotions underneath his veneer, impassive for all his attention to the image on the television screen. He's not relating to the girl he's with, and they're both almost naked. They have a strangely intense sexual and interpersonal relationship, as suggested by the primitive sculpture, even though they seem to exist in separate emotional worlds, or at least very remote from one another.*

EF: They're being witnessed by the fetish object. I agree with what you're saying. I think that's exactly how they were. The object supplies the details of emotional turmoil.

One thing that became a problem for me as a painter, which is in general a rather essential problem for depiction, is the question or role of detail. I found that I could establish a kind of hierarchy whose terms were signified by objects that had a psychological function. It was these things that really interested me. I felt they conveyed the essential meaning of the pictures. It was displaced onto them.

These things were depicted in various degrees, that is, they were nominally "realistic." These degrees of depiction filled out the fictional space in which the drama of the picture occurs. I might find that I'm interested in the torso, thighs and face of a character, and I devote a lot of time to getting them right. I have some idea of what it means to get them right. But then I don't care about the vase on the table, except that it seems an object is required there. My problem is to determine how many brushstrokes it would take to make a vase appear like a vase. How simply can you depict a table that everyone knows is a table, without getting involved in the kind of absolute, realistic material quality of that table? So, in a sense, such objects are like props, part of a stage set. But I think I put most of my emphasis on the action of the people.

DK: *Did you learn to paint in art school?*

EF: I finished at the California Institute of the Arts.

DK: *When you say finished, do you mean you didn't begin there?*

EF: Right. I began at Phoenix Junior College. I flunked out of a small midwestern Presbyterian college outside of Pittsburgh. That was about 1967. I was on my way to becoming a hippie, so I was pretty exhausted by school and I dropped out. I flunked and quit. And then I went to San Francisco and tried to be a hippie for a while. I went back to live with my family, who had by then moved to Phoenix.

DK: *What year was that?*

EF: Oh, sometime in 1967 or 1968. In 1968 I enrolled at Phoenix Junior College simply so that I could meet people. This was after living at home for a year in Phoenix without knowing anybody and being very depressed. It wasn't a pleasant time around the house. I didn't want to take any academic courses because I had done so miserably in college. I just had no patience for it, so I thought I'd take an art class because that's easier. And I found I got very involved in that. I think what hooked me on art was that making it was the first time in my life that I could be alone in my room or wherever and be fully concentrated for long periods of time. I'd never had that experience before. I always either watched TV or sort of zoned out or inhabited some kind of dream space, without ever being focused. Making art was the first time I was seriously using my mind, seriously conscious.

Being alone was a big deal for me. I was undistracted, focused. And so I thought, "Gee, this is great." Also—this was 1968 and a very provincial situation—there was a teacher there, a guy named Merrill McHampton, who was a very significant art teacher for me. He was involved in contemporary art through pop art, which was his entrance to it. He encouraged us to make art that was like antiart, to play around with scale and with common popular images. Above all, it was his antiestablishment position that was compelling. It seemed an easy position to have. It was easy to be a wild person in that small situation.

Actually, the next year, I outgrew Phoenix Junior College and went to Arizona State University, which was considered to be the real thing. Now I'd become a real artist. This was where things would start getting tough, where I'd take some real courses, where the teachers were real artists, etc. I was very fortunate in that situation to have a graduate school assistant for my first year of painting, a guy named Bill Swang, who brought the metaphysical dimension in art to me, brought abstraction, through Kandinsky and Gorky and the abstract expressionists. He gave art a kind of spiritual intonation. He introduced mystery as an important element. I try to retain it, but not in an abstract context, not as a metaphysical mystery.

DK: *How long were you a hippie?*

EF: Not very long. I wasn't a very good hippie.

DK: *What do you mean?*

EF: Well, I was a little bit off. My hair didn't grow long until after I had stopped being a hippie; I was a hippie with short hair. I got my hair cut right before I caught on to the whole thing, and by that time I was already moving to another place. I had these kind of nerdy glasses that I wore the whole time, and I was wearing bell-bottoms or moccasins with bells on them and ridiculous stuff like that. I never quite got the look right. On top of that, I tried very hard to take literally what I had been told, that you had to love everybody. I was into passive acceptance of every life-style and every attitude. It was finally intolerable. Most of the other hippies were completely boring. Their life was repetitive. It was a dumb fantasy.

DK: *Do you have brothers and sisters?*

EF: Yes.

DK: *Are you close to them?*

EF: Yes and no. I have two sisters and a brother. One sister is eleven months older than I am. And I have a sister who is six years younger and a brother who is nine years younger. We're close in the sense of being friendly. I'm closest to my older sister, because eleven months' difference is basically none. But we don't have similar life-styles.

DK: *Are your parents still alive?*

EF: My mother is dead. My father remarried.

DK: *Were you particularly close to your mother or father? I ask you this because your work directly comments on the character of contemporary interpersonality, and we know its roots are in family relationships. I would also like to know what your parents thought about you becoming an artist.*

EF: Well, my father wanted me to go into business, which I later found out he meant in a halfhearted way. He believed that if you didn't know what to do, you should go into business.

DK: *Was he a businessman himself?*

25

EF: He was a salesman. He thought that if you were shiftless, you could always go into business. Then you'd have a little background and you could do whatever you wanted. I guess he got stuck there. My mother was a very creative person, but extremely frustrated.

DK: I heard that she was an artist.

EF: She tried a lot of things. She tried writing. She tried being an artist. It was tragic, because she could never realize what she wanted. She knew more than she could realize. I grew up with a similar attitude. I believed you could not get where you wanted to creatively. So I never took myself seriously as a creative artist. But I always admired her. We didn't go to art museums a lot. On school trips, I went to the Met and the Guggenheim. I always preferred the natural history museum. I didn't really grow up in an art environment. My mother was happy I went back to school when I wanted to be an artist. My father was not. He thought I had made a big mistake. What the hell was I doing? To him, it looked like I would never leave home. I would never make any money being an artist.

An interesting thing happened when I started to become successful. I began sending him reviews, thinking that he would understand what I was doing. I knew he didn't appreciate the work, but he could appreciate my name in print. I thought it would be a way of drawing us closer. The experience was gratifying. I found out over the course of several years of sending him things that, in fact, he understood what I was doing in my art, and had understood it all along. He had been using my art as a way of coming to terms with a lot of the pain that we all suffered through my mother's alcoholism.

It happened at one point that I had had a show in the Sable Castelli Gallery in Toronto, and got this fantastic review. It was a full-page review based on one painting, which the critic really went into. He was very moved by the painting. I was really pleased by the review. I sent it to my father with the image of the picture. Several months later I was visiting my father and he said that he had sent copies to all the other children and that he was very surprised to get a letter back from my younger sister, who was very upset with it. She had asked in this letter how he could send the review and image around. She said he was not a good father. He was not protecting her from the harsh memories of the past. The painting was of a woman possessed—a woman in a driveway, surrounded by neighborhood dogs, some passive and cute, some aggressive and sort of holding her down. That is, she's passed out on the driveway. There's an empty glass next to her. And there's a boy trying to ease her away from those dogs. My sister was very upset. My father sent her back a letter and he showed me both my sister's letter and his response. In his letter back to her he laid out how he had been using my art all along to come to terms with some very difficult feelings. It was really fantastic.

DK: *Are you close to your father?*

EF: I think we've become closer.

DK: *What did you do after you finished school in California?*

EF: I went to Chicago. I went there because I was afraid to go to New York. I had never been to Chicago and I thought it would be like New York. It would train you for living in the big city. The thing about growing up in the suburbs is that you're out there because your parents believe it's not safe to bring children up in the city. In the suburbs you always consider yourself essentially innocent or a child at heart or something like that. The city is this place you're not supposed to go to. To move to New York would be to confront that idea. So I moved to Chicago because I wasn't really ready to deal with it. Still, I wanted to find myself. I worked as a guard at the Museum of Contemporary Art. I was lucky to get a job there, and I stayed in Chicago for two years, from 1972 to 1974.

DK: *Were you painting then?*

EF: I was painting all the time. The nice thing about Chicago art was that it was modernist, but in a surrealist vein. This was very different from Cal Arts, which was very New York–oriented. Also, at Cal Arts they thought that painting was dead. So anyone who painted was a necrophiliac—perversely fascinated with corpses. The dynamic person at Cal Arts was John Baldessari, who was really a significant teacher for us. A whole group of artists important today, such as David Salle, came out of Cal Arts and studied with John. Paul Brach was also an interesting teacher. He was a second- or third-generation abstract expressionist, full of Cedar Bar stories. He filled us with belief in legendary New York painters. Allan Hackman was also very important to me. He was a very young, miraculous abstractionist who had three years of skyrocketing success. He was a lyrical painter who sold everything and made a lot of money. He was able to buy a big farm upstate. He got a teaching job at the most prestigious art school to open at the time. And so forth. He was very dynamic and energetic. But during that whole time, we watched his career go right down the drain, because lyrical abstractionism got pigeonholed and couldn't sustain itself. So we got an ambivalent picture of this mythical place, New York, on the one side giving so much and on the other a harsh reality. It was enough to scare the hell out of you.

At the time, I did abstract painting. Constructivist-type stuff, the formalist field thing, full of geometric forms. Not very good at all. So I went to Chicago and found something completely different. Images were very popular there. It was a permissive place. Also, Chicago people are about the friendliest people I've ever met. Unbelievably nice. It's not competitive in the New York way at all. They become your friends. You share a sense of well-being, which is amazing. It's amazing to share anything at all in the art world. In New York, you're friends because you feel you're in this prison together. In Chicago, friendship is based on a feeling of security. That was very helpful.

I began to play around with images. Then I retreated back to abstraction, but I had acquired a narrative sense. I started reading about architecture and mythology. In the late sixties primitivism was very popular, especially American Indian primitivism. I began to work with that, but it was very difficult in the context of formal abstraction. By the time I went to Nova Scotia in 1975 to teach in the art college there, I was working more directly with images which I understood narratively. I used architectural forms identified as houses as much as shapes.

DK: *Was there anybody in Chicago or Nova Scotia that influenced your work?*

EF: No. In Chicago I didn't really meet artists. I knew young artists like myself, whom I hung around with. I didn't really get to know any of the older, more established artists like Jim Nutt. But I saw a lot of their work.

In Nova Scotia I was thrown back into a New York focus, a late modernist aesthetic. Nova Scotia's reputation was based on the fact that, very early, it had shown and promoted such people as Carl Andre and Lawrence Weiner, and Europeans like Joseph Beuys and Penck. The school was famous because of its support of conceptual and performance art. However, they couldn't ignore the fact that sixty percent of their student body wanted to paint, which is why they hired me. They didn't know anything about me, but I was recommended by Allan Hackman, whom they respected. They wanted someone young and energetic who could service the majority of their students.

DK: *Did you feel like an outsider there? You seem to describe yourself as an outsider at Cal Arts. Is this a general feeling you have?*

EF: Well, I've often felt myself in the curious position of being a minority working within the majority. However, I never took an oppositional position, emphasizing that I was a painter. Nonetheless, it was something that filled me with pride and gave me lots of insights. I never felt intellectually competitive with the anti-painters, but their arguments and resistance helped me define my sense of painting. At Nova Scotia I wasn't treated as an outsider, but it was a peculiar situation. After a couple of years, I was actually treated as very central to the college's program. That probably was connected to the fact that taste in art was changing. Painting was beginning to be talked about. Artists like Jon Borofsky and Joel Shapiro were very important in bringing about the postminimalist psychological image.

DK: *How long did you teach in Nova Scotia?*

EF: Four years. I left in 1978 to come to New York.

DK: *Did you have a teaching job in New York?*

EF: No. I came just to come. I reached a crisis point in Nova Scotia. There were serious policy decisions that were being made. It was the kind of experimental school where every semester you change the name of the program, because you can never define what it is. Things had been coming to a head because of that. The school faculty was mostly made up of people my age. Many of them were graduate students from the college itself, who were reaching a point in their work and intellectual life where they were rejecting their teachers. So there was a lot of friction. I myself had a choice to make. At first I didn't want to leave. I was terrified of going to New York. Nova Scotia has a very monastic attitude about art even though it was obsessed with New York. The attitude was paradoxical. If you had a show there, you had gone over to the other side, violated the monasticism. Yet the college brought in all these high-profile New York artists, whom it admired. It was a very difficult situation. I thought I was going to stay and fight it out. But then I met April Gornick, and she wanted very much to go to New York. And so, with her courage, we left. Gary Kennedy [president of the Nova Scotia College of Art and Design] said he fired me. I don't remember that he did. I left.

DK: *What kind of paintings did you make when you first arrived in New York?*

EF: I had started doing glassine drawings using overlays. They were fictionalized narratives based on family structure. Just as, in 1975, I started to make a transition from abstraction to figuration, so now I was moving from simple figuration to complex narrative. I quit abstraction because each painting had begun to seem like the last one. I began to feel the same thing when I got into figural images, so I thought a good strategy would be to find a way of generating a lot of work by working off a core narrative. Each thing that I did would illustrate and extend the basic narrative. I could go off in any direction as long as it pointed back to the narrative that I established at the start. After a while, the works began to connect, revealing more about the narrative, which never quite totalized. I started with the family matrix, exploring the relationships between father and mother, brother and sister, husband and wife, son and daughter, and their various permutations. Couples and groups especially interested me. I was still working on glassine. I was very afraid of academic realism. I wanted to come out of modernism, but I was using transparent overlays related to it. I was showing how the picture was constructed, and I started structuring my pictures so I could represent everything. I decided that chairs, tables and beds—whatever was the backdrop for the settings— should be painted in a flat, black, isometric design to signify place abstractly. In contrast, the body, especially the head, was articulated psychologically. The work became a composite of body language and abstract design. This was my code, and it got complex. At times I didn't even attach the head to the body, which I painted in black, linear outline. It took me a long time to give up that code and just work with the figures. When you're young and afraid, you rigidly hold to a code.

DK: *How long did the code last?*

EF: I started the glassines in 1976 and '77. I stopped doing them in 1982, making a few until 1984. After a couple of years, I began to attach the head to the body and I began to be less dogmatic about the kind of furniture I pictured. I began to make a specific chair rather than an isometric one. One painting, on plywood, of a boy's toy boat, was an important transition to psychological narrative. I decided that I'd paint the boy's boat to suggest a story in which the boy's father was a fisherman and the boy imitated his father with the toy boat. The painting turned out to be red, yellow and blue—absolutely reductive. It was an important transitional work for me.

DK: What happened next?

EF: Let me go back to the toy boat painting, which I brought to New York. The glassine paintings were still modernist to some degree because they revealed their structure and material. At the same time, they were narrative and psychological. So this painting, which I had intended to be illustrative, turned out to be beautiful, which I hadn't expected. I wasn't working for a quality of beauty. But it also had an extraordinary light in it. It was very moving. That compelled me to think more seriously about painting on canvas and in a more fully developed way than in the schematic linear style I had been working with. I was also extremely nervous because history was pushing toward academic realism. I knew that if I went directly into representational painting, I would have to give up even the little bit of modernism I had cleverly used in the glassines. But I was compelled by this one painting [of the boy's toy boat]. I decided I would try to do a figurative painting. I had never painted one, and I wasn't schooled to. I had had no drawing classes. Drawing was frowned on at Cal Arts. At best, it was reluctantly zoned. We actually had one drawing class I'll never forget. It was about 1970, the peak of crazed liberal ideas about education and self-development. Do your own thing. No rules. No history. We had this drawing class that Allan Hackman had put together. I arrived late. It started around nine or ten in the morning, but I couldn't get there until eleven. I walked into the studio and everybody was naked. Right! *Everybody* was naked. Half the people were covered with paint. They rolled around on the ground, on pieces of brown paper that they had torn off a roll. The two models are sitting in the corner absolutely still, bored to tears. Everybody else was throwing stuff around and had climbed up onto the roof and jumped into buckets of paint. It was an absolute zoo.

DK: *It was late modernism.*

EF: Right. It was an idea about what a drawing class might be, not one. With this experience in my memory, I was very nervous about starting in on a representational painting without knowing how to paint the figure. But I thought, "What the hell, I can do that." At Cal Arts we were taught to believe that we were all professionals. We could do anything we wanted to. But our minds developed at a faster rate than our facility, because they didn't teach technique at Cal Arts. Our facility didn't do very well at all. But we had this sense of knowing what we were doing, knowing what history was, knowing what strategies were, knowing that there was this great purpose behind what we were doing. There was also the belief that you could educate yourself in public. You could be real smart about art if you could defend articulately what you were doing. You could be bad publicly and it would be okay if you were clever about being bad. With that in mind, I tried to make figurative painting. The first painting I did—the first one that survived—was *Sleepwalker.* It was the painting of the boy masturbating in the wading pool. That painting started out as a sensational idea. I wanted to shock an audience. I wanted to make something pornographic. A lot of the artists—Longo, Goldstein, Salle—were already working with images from cultural and sociopolitical history. Historical and cultural imagery had a lot of power attached to the image itself, apart from what you did to it. A portrait of Hitler or any kind of allusion to that aspect of World War II had instant currency. You didn't have to develop it any further. It was powerful in itself.

DK: *It was forbidden.*

EF: It was forbidden. And, of course, they were working on it precisely because they could render it in such an ambiguous way that the audience didn't know why it was being called up. There wasn't a morality attached to it. It was simply a portrait of Hitler. What do you do with it?

DK: Did you use the image of the figure masturbating the same way?

EF: Yes. It was taboo yet obvious. It also involved the idea that calling up power implies that you can wield it. You can handle it, and perhaps are powerful yourself. Roberta Smith once said to me that she had a lot of questions about it because she thought it might be a short cut to getting power in art. That was part of it, but I wanted to make a painting that would deal with the taboo and be quasi-pornographic. I wanted to try it. And so I painted this boy masturbating. It was a tremendous struggle for me. I didn't even know how to paint full-fledged figures. I was trying to learn that as well. The choice of image turned out to be a lot more loaded than I thought it would be. My relationship to it was a lot more complex than I had initially imagined it would be. When I finished the painting, I found that I had painted a sympathetic image. It wasn't simply a trick to get power. It wasn't a powerful image detached from emotional context and history. I painted this sympathetic image of a profound moment in a child's psychological and sexual life. The painting had two beach chairs in it. It was at night, which was way I called it *Sleepwalker.* The lighting makes you feel like there's something incongruous about the scene. The kid stands in a kiddie pool. Why is he there? It was almost as though he were sleepwalking through a ritual. The night light suggests—symbolizes—the unconscious character of the act. The two chairs represent the parental authorities. But they are absent —the chairs are empty. This whole statement of self-pleasure and self-sufficiency and a kind of self-identification was unconscious. It was also a dry run, because the witnesses weren't there to witness. I was creating something far more complex than I had thought it would be. That led me to try to explore some other areas that had been taboo or considered taboo, such as the relationship between blacks and whites. I was interested in the sexual mystery and question of prowess involved in the relationship. I was also interested in the potentially sexual relationships between parents and children.

DK: *One of the things one notices in many images of that period, and continuing to this day, is that an adolescent figure is the psychological center of the piece. Is that a correct statement?*

EF: Yes. The point of view of the work is of a child looking at an adult situation. The more I painted, the more closely the work pinpointed the moment of transition that puberty is about. It is the transition from innocence to knowledge. I paint a kind of suburban Garden of Eden in which sexual awakening and self-discovery occur.

DK: *Carnal knowledge and self-consciousness develop at the same time.*

EF: Exactly. That's a very good way of thinking about it.

DK: *A lot of your work seems to show a great deal of self-consciousness about being an artist. You have painted a wonderful self-portrait of yourself as an old painter who seems to be masturbating as he is painting. The paint itself, as in many of your works, has an uncanny sexual quality. The multipaneled work you have here* [Saigon Minnesota] *shows a certain self-consciousness about the making of an object. Is your quasi-modernist "constructivism" creeping back in?*

EF: Yes, the self-consciousness is part of my reluctance to create works with a look that could be regarded as beautiful. It's also part of my reluctance about craft.

DK: *Is it also related to your peculiar fusion of the photographic and the painterly? There's an odd tension between them in your pictures.*

EF: Yes, it's an important issue. I'm not sure that I can satisfactorily explain it. I am absolutely torn precisely between "realistic" image and touch. I want to establish a kind of comfortable relationship between them. I'm drawn in by material rendering. I can get obsessed with trying to create a sense of material or flesh, with the way to render a thigh or stomach. At the same time, I want to pull back and not do the whole surface the way a Géricault would. I want it, but I'm reluctant to do it. I want to be indulgent but I'm afraid to be. It's about being puritan and sensually abandoned at once. It's antistylistic and antiflashy while being stylish and flashy. The realism of Manet and Winslow Homer, both of whom I admire, has something of the same powerful ambivalence. It gives just enough to make you think you're looking at something real, which is the painting equivalent of photography. You don't spend a lot of time thinking about the mechanism of how it was made. It's different from wanting to be so perfect that you end up meditating on how perfect it is. I want to give just enough muscle tone or flesh tone, enough of a dose of life, that you don't think about how it was made. You just say, this is a figure sitting down. That's the kind of realism I admire, and that I'm trying to achieve. At the same time, I want to rely on the force of the narrative, the sensuous thrill or shock or subtlety of the actual moment. This can be strongly conveyed through the indulgence of the paint. I want to create a picture in which one can give oneself to the paint as well as to the image.

DK: You were talking about making an art object. Would this apply to the way you "make" a subject matter as well?

EF: I don't think so. That's an interesting contradiction. I want people to feel they're present at a scene they shouldn't be at, and don't want to be at. This is something that can't be created by painting, however basic. The scene has to be taken in very fast and left as quickly, and then slowly digested. If people have to start examining this or that detail, they miss the full point of the picture, which is that they're a kind of accomplice in it, an unwilling witness to the event. I want them to think about that, not just how the picture is made.

DK: Are you more comfortable painting the figure than you once were? Do you feel you have mastered the body language?

EF: My paintings are more and more about that. Also, my work is less and less specific about what is taking place. It's much more subtle and ambiguous than it once was. It's propelled more by the body language of the figures than by anything they're doing. The faces and bodies are more integrated into a single psychological language than they once were.

DK: Your recent works seem to divide into images with many figures—big group scenes—and those with very few figures, often only one figure.

EF: Right.

DK: Do you prefer one kind to the other?

EF: I think my big dream is to repaint *The Night Watch.* I love the idea of that kind of scale, of public painting and the variety of personalities that are there all at the same moment, witnessing an event. I like that a lot. I don't think I ever made a painting that has as many people in it as I thought I could put in it. It takes a lot of energy to put a lot of figures in. Also, I think my work is basically about compression rather than expansion. And so what starts out as a lot ends up being less than I originally aspired to. So I don't know if I'll ever make it to *The Night Watch*—to a cast of thousands. I really don't have the extravagance. Or, hopefully, not the kitschiness.

DK: Is a Hollywood as well as a Rembrandt sensibility involved? Are they intertwined in your work?

EF: Well, I don't know. There's definitely a sense of film in my work.

DK: And of spectacle.

EF: Yes.

DK: *How individualized do you want your figures to be within the context of the Hollywood/Rembrandt spectacle? Do you even think of them as individuals?*

EF: I try to. But as part of a narrative.

DK: *But there's a curious antinarrative quality to your works. It's increasingly hard to place the story. It becomes more of a subtle psycho-dramatic interaction between the figures than a specific event. Even the sexual story seems almost incidental to a more primary tension operating between the figures. Does this make sense?*

EF: Well, I'm not interested in narrative in the strict sense, as a kind of linear progression. I try to create a narrative whose elements have no secure, ascribed meanings so that an effect of greater pregnancy of meaning and moment can be generated than in customary straightforward narrative. For example, in *Sleep-walker,* the chairs are simultaneously chairs and represent the absence of people. They have no simple meaning. In a sense, their ambiguous meaning is itself the narrative. The kiddie pool is important because it implies the boy is too old—yet emotionally not too old—to be there. Why is he there? Raising such questions is the narrative. Painting is most potent when nothing has been nailed down. You bring to it associations that lead you forward from and backward into the moment of the picture.

Now, what I think is important about painting in this narrative manner is that it does something photography, film, and theater cannot do. Film takes place within linear time. Painting is a frozen moment. It's frozen, to some extent, the way photography is frozen, except—and it makes all the difference—that photography is mechanistic in a way that doesn't allow the audience to fully believe the poignancy of the frozen moment because they know it's completely changed in a split second. The photograph has edited the moment down. That leads to some suspicion of it. In painting, you always sense the painter building up to the moment and its possible meaning, so that you identify with the maker, finding yourself with him at the point of revelation. You participate with him in the frozen point of clarity. Because of this, painting is less cynical than photography. In painting, both the viewer and artist are less removed from the object made.

DK: *In speaking about* Sleepwalker, *you mentioned the implied parental presence. In a number of your works, while the scenes are often very full, there is always the sense—and I think this is part of their pregnancy —of a hidden presence. Am I correct in thinking this? For me, it adds to the sense of great expectation in the images. What I admire about your works is the way this sense of a lurking, invisible presence seems to get stronger and stronger the more clearly visible everything becomes.*

EF: I do try to create the effect of something unsaid. I wonder if it's fair to ask how I go about trying to generate a sense of haunting unconscious presence. I'm pretty self-conscious about my strategies, but they all exist to make you aware of this thing inside me. I get it out onto the canvas, but never completely. I know the painting is finished when I become its audience. I try to paint this externalization process. This is why I don't work from the model, which is already completely external. I'm not interested in conforming to the already totally visible. I want the viewer to experience my process of externalization, my enactment.

DK: *This is why the pictures feel intimate despite their larger-than-life realistic character.*

EF: The viewer is part of the intimacy, that's for sure. What he feels is desire. It's desire that takes the form of a big question mark. It is precisely that self-consciousness about desire that is the mystery of the works. What happens in them happens because of desire, which is the mystery I want to paint.

DK: *You often show a figure alone in a kind of vacuum. As you develop, you seem to paint more and more empty space, no matter how large or small the figure is. Is it correct to say that emptiness interests you, from the empty chairs in* Sleepwalker *to the empty room the girl with her Labrador dog inhabits? Does the empty space generate a sense of unconscious expectation or imply someone present only in the unconscious of the figure?*

EF: It is a reductivist theatrical device. My figures are set on a stage. The objects are props to signify a place. Everything takes place in the theatrical or fictional void of the stage, which signals its emotional depth or possibilities. The pictures deal with the tense relationships between people, the potential for action between them, which could be sexual or violent or absurd or pitiful, or all of them at once. Each is a carefully calculated psycho-dramatic gamble that needs vast emotional space to unfold in.

The figures are like dice thrown on a gaming table. One doesn't know what will turn up, what relationship they'll have. Each picture is about a potential occurrence that stops short and is not completely predictable. *Daddy's Girl,* for example. It was a very difficult painting for me to make. I started out with the idea that the public expected a sort of naughtiness from me, a difficult moment. But I didn't necessarily want to give it. I didn't necessarily want to depict a "negative" relationship. So I started out with the image of an older man, a father or grandfather, fondling, in a very affectionate way, his child or grandchild. The question was, what's wrong with flesh-on-flesh? What's wrong with a man hugging a little girl? I tried to keep the relationship positive, upbeat, despite the expectation of my public. I struggled with the image. Everything about it made me nervous. I kept thinking of how to reassure people that there was nothing wrong in the relationship. I initially put in other people to convey this. They could watch and guard the couple, keep them from unwholesomeness. I got so desperately lost in the painting that I even painted myself in as a guardian. The man and the girl are on a patio. I put myself at a table in the back, just looking out. The artist's presence was surely going to be enough to prevent. . . . I had a gardener walking through, carrying a hose. Another person would assure that this thing wouldn't go in the wrong direction, the direction that everyone unconsciously wanted it to go in. But there should be nothing wrong with the couple as such. I finally put in a glass of iced tea. It was the last thing I put in the picture. I put it equidistant between the viewer and the characters. You are the one who is going to assure that nothing wrong occurs or has occurred or will occur. You are also the one who is aware of the negative potential of the scene in the first place.

What I realized was that nothing is wrong with what's happening. There's nothing wrong with the way the man holds the child. He's not sexually aroused. He's not fondling her in an erotic way, not touching her private parts. He's just hugging her. Yet you don't trust that, precisely because they're alone. You know there's no way of really stopping something from happening, or that something may be going on unconsciously between them. I try to make the viewer conscious of that.

DK: *That is, you make the viewer conscious of his perverse and nasty expectations.*

EF: Right.

DK: *You put the viewer in a terrible, unresolvable, ambivalent position.*

EF: Naughty me. Yes, it's true.

DK: *There's an uncanny continuity between* Daddy's Girl *and* Birthday Boy. *There, you show the boy isolated and melancholy between the question mark of the woman's legs, the question mark of desire. In* Daddy's Girl *the figures are also very isolated. Do you mean to emphasize emotional solitude in your work?*

EF: I don't start out making a specific meaning occur in the painting. I discover the meaning of the painting as I paint and upon reflection. But what you're picking up is that I take the child's point of view in both paintings, and it's a lonely point of view. I try to see the scene as a child would, and the child—especially the child in every adult—is isolated and melancholy.

You can study a child's face and perceive in it the character of its exposure or overexposure to the female—the mother. That overexposure is reflected in *Birthday Boy* in his incestuous situation. I also raise the question of child abuse. You can see it on the boy's face because it's not an unencumbered, purely erotic moment that I've depicted. There's a lot of ambiguity—complexity, difficulty—on the child's face. He's not exactly joyfully celebrating the occasion of his and the woman's nakedness. She's an ambiguous parental presence. It does connect to *Daddy's Girl*. The two kids face the audience.

DK: Is there a political point to your pictures? Are they meant to comment critically on contemporary American society? You seem aware not only of the sexual abuse of children, but of the youth culture. Earlier you spoke of the profound frustration in the world of satisfaction which the suburbs are supposed to be. Your pictures can be understood as a devastating critique of the big lie of suburban life and the suburban ideal that is so central to America. This seems to me the full, critical weight of your realism.

EF: Right. But there is no hidden political agenda in my work. There's no specific doctrine I'm pushing to change things. There is criticism and a kind of analysis, but no proposal for an alternative. I don't know any.

DK: I assume you're dealing with a specifically American world. I sense that you're determined to expose America. This is why I would call your art critical realism.

EF: That's true. I'm not talking at large. I'm talking about a peculiarly American kind of contradiction and dissatisfaction. But I don't mean to imply there's an American solution to it, as though America was this miraculous place that could solve all the problems of life. I'm describing an American tragedy, and suggesting that it has to be addressed by the American public. It's not just tragedy; it's a specifically American tragedy, which tells us something about the spiritual dilemma of American life, the spiritual dilemma of suburban life and the surburban dream.

DK: *How does* Daddy's Girl *show this dilemma?*

EF: Well, the house in the picture is a wonderful contemporary modern house, exquisite and expensive. The older people who live in it are very well-to-do. They belong to the affluent society. My earlier works dealt with more middle-class people. Now they're much wealthier. And they're still struggling with the interpersonal.

DK: *They have the luxury of paying close attention to their feelings and desires, and worrying about the character of their relationships.*

EF: I see that as a curse, not a luxury. Their prosperity doesn't fill out their lives. They fill it out by worrying their interpersonal life to death. For me, their suffering and unhappiness is more cultural, even mythological—almost epic—in scale, rather than just ordinarily social. It's a struggle for self-identification and self-knowledge.

DK: *Could you clarify the difference between the cultural and social?*

EF: I'll try to. I think of "social" as involving the particulars of daily life, from ordinary interpersonal to specifically political interaction. The "cultural" involves the full psychohistorical sense of ourselves. Social life takes place in the present. Cultural life involves a more complicated sense of time. It deals with the way we mythologize ourselves in images and beliefs.

DK: *Can you say more about what you mean by the tragic?*

EF: I think of it as a matter of internal conflict. It means there's

43

something inherently wrong that can destroy those experiencing it. I think my ambition is to show that tragedy operates even in supposedly ordinary, middle-class life. The American middle class isn't able to come to terms with the contradictions generated by its ambitions, expressed particularly in the dream of suburban life. So it remains fundamentally tragic. It can't escape tragedy. You can have a picture-book-perfect house and still suffer feelings of abandonment that you don't expect to have. That's a specifically American-type tragedy. It is harder to accept or believe in death and murky feelings in the suburbs, even though they occur there. Americans have to learn that even if you live prosperously in the suburbs you are permitted to publicly express grief and discomfort and embarrassment. You can experience the difficult emotions. I found through experience that there's no way to celebrate or mourn death in a serious public way in suburban America. It threatened the ambition to have everything be perfect and calm and to be one of the beautiful people. Suburbanites don't believe you can get knowledge out of these uncomfortable, awkward events. Suburbanites have lost both the heroic and the tragic sense of self. They don't believe the heroic and the tragic exist, or should exist.

DK: Suppose a certain kind of critic was to say that your pictures are literature, not painting. How would you respond to that old distinction?

EF: I would say that I don't think it is true. The best paintings have achieved significance and authority through drama, including the drama of their paint. I personally have tried to articulate that moment of poignancy that causes you to have an experience that you *must* reflect on. I use my paint process to cut through meanings that are *supposed* to be there in order to get that precise moment at which meaning occurs. For me, this is a process of going backward. Analyzing—not even analyzing, but feeling—my relationship to this or that thing. What keeps my work vivid and keeps it in the minds of people is precisely the empathy with which I project these very dramatic, difficult interpersonal relationships.

I'm not cynical about them. I'm looking at a human condition and human behavior under certain conditions. This is why I side with the child. It's more vulnerable, human. I prefer the child masturbating to the authority that says masturbating is wrong. I prefer the tragic person to the person who denies his own tragedy.

DK: Earlier you spoke about your ambiguous relationship to modernism, which would accept the separation of painting and literature as basic. For it, authentic painting is not literary. Would you call yourself a postmodernist? Is part of what it is to be a postmodernist to think this separation is nonsense?

EF: I'm not interested in the modernism self-consciously concerned with the nature of art. I like the modernism that would deal with what I'd call the subconsciousness of the art object. I'm fascinated by my own process of thinking and discovering, and I like art objects that reflect those processes. What was compelling to me about the glassine drawings was that their method of construction, by a technique of overlay, reflected a mental decision-making process. What interests me about my narrative paintings is what I identify with in the scene. It could be a lamp or a person or a gesture. I'm interested in amplifying that empathic feeling, making it and its rationale as self-evident as possible. My current use of many panels is part of that effort at amplification, at making every nuance of feeling evident. I don't make multipaneled paintings because they're formally important or novel at the moment. I use one panel to bring into view what is offscreen or off the set, out of the "basic" rectangle, so to speak. If the basic rectangle is a modernist idea of the structure of the work, I'm postmodernist. I want to fill out the basic rectangle with what seems peripheral but is more insidiously basic. I want the narrative context which dissolves the formally basic. I am interested in a more complete view, because I find it more true emotionally.

DK: You have mentioned the various objects you are drawn to depict. One of the most startling objects you render is the African fetish figure.

45

Various critics have commented on its strategic emotional as well as physical importance in various works. It appears like a strange yet insidiously relevant non sequitur. Sometimes the primitive figure seems to come fantastically alive. Could you comment on your use of this object?

EF: It's not unconnected to postmodernism. The artists of my generation feel that you can borrow freely from any time and place to construct your own image. So-called pluralism means that you can locate yourself in different periods of time. My work seems to come out of the nineteenth century, but it also uses twentieth-century primitivism. Other artists go back to the fifties or surrealism or the thirties. All these different styles and philosophies based on different stylistic advances are available for use. It's like the universe has curled back on itself and become full of possibilities that were half-realized but still have a long way to go. In that sense, I think I'm a postmodernist, and my use of tribal artifacts is postmodernist. But I don't think postmodernism means a rejection of modernism, nor does it mean eclecticism. It's highly selective to a purpose. It really means empathizing with the myth of a stylistic period and working within that myth, reenacting it in a new context.

I began to use the fetish object in the seventies, when I was looking for religion.

DK: Personally speaking?

EF: Yes. I believed that art came from religion and I didn't have one. I don't think we had one culturally. Religion was eroded. It was tied to social form rather than theological concerns or spiritual discipline. And art had moved off into its own kind of self-righteously self-referential thing. So, initially, I tried to get religion by borrowing other religions. I borrowed it from primitive things because it was clear that they—art objects—were completely integrated with religious life. But these objects were ultimately very dissatisfying. They created in me a sense of longing. I clearly couldn't be a primitive. The time isn't right, is it? What survived was the wreckage of my search. The artifacts I use are the detritus of the spiritual ship that had sunk. In part they signify my disappointment.

But I became a bit more hardened and perhaps cynical about their use. I abandoned my spiritual search and focused on the contemporary problem of the use of primitive relics. I began to look at the people who had no religion, and at the emptiness of their lives, which they often fill with art, especially primitive art, to give it a boost. I mean religion in a general way, not specifically Judeo-Christian religion. I think of religion as something that helps us understand ourselves in relation to the world. This is why the absence of religion was so devastating for these people. It was responsible for their emptiness, because they had no way to explain themselves. The fetish objects represent the possibility of such an "explanation." They are a way of articulating moments of profound experience that can't be explained away. They are a handle on what the empty people don't know how to get a handle on.

Also, I started to work with the relationship of blacks and whites and began to introduce "black" objects. They represented the bizarreness of alien relationships. They're also trophies from my travels. Morocco was a very dramatic place for me to visit. You saw naked people socializing on the beaches. Naked white people and fully clothed black Africans walking along the edge of the water, selling their wares. Coming from an American background where there's such a taboo about black men and white women— black sexual power, the white man's fear of losing his woman to that power—it seemed very strange. A taboo was casually, implicitly broken. You could see the white woman naked. It was a free exchange visually in an incredibly tight, controlled society that would prevent any open, explicit sexual relationship. The fetish object represents the tragic exoticism of this fantasy situation—its absolute bizarreness.

DK: Was there any particular painting in which you feel that that sense of bizarreness is particularly strong?

EF: One is *Cargo Cults*, in which you see a white woman and a black woman walking down the beach. They are being howled at by a large white male figure seen from behind. He is naked and hooting at them, while his sailor buddies are sitting on the beach like an invasion force. This is their beachhead and they're in the process of possessing it. They may be from a cruise line or luxury ship, so their invasion may be frivolous. But they are being confronted by a shaman off to the side. He is trying to ward them away but, of course, in the context he's overwhelmed, and in fact looks like a bag lady. It's as though he has almost no impetus in the face of these guys, who are completely oblivious to his otherness. They're about sameness and male bonding.

Another painting is *Slumber Party*. I used a fetish figure I had seen a photograph of. It's such a fantastic and bizarre figure, double-headed and with quadruple arms. It seemed very expressionistic and dramatic. I used it in the context of this scene to convey something hidden. You're looking at a white boy in the attic environment of the maid, who is probably a black woman. She's starting to get undressed. There is a sleeping bag on the floor as well as a bed. It's not clear whether he's coming up to stay for comfort or companionship and will sleep in the sleeping bag, or whether he'll get in bed with her and have some kind of sexual experience, perhaps an initiation, into whatever. By decontextualizing the fetish object, taking it out of its culture, it loses its power to some extent. Yet the offstage light and TV light make its shadow huge. The shadow spreads across the whole room and spotlights the fetish figure. It is as if the figure has come alive again. By anecdotalizing it, as it were, I gave it fresh, bizarre power. I reconstituted its religious power so that the scene wasn't entirely empty. I used the figure to signify its tragic potential. The figure itself is tragic because of its absurdity. We look at it, but we don't really believe in it, so it doesn't exist as a power. But in another light, it just might secretly control the scene.

DK: *Does it represent a projection of the unconscious of the people in the scene?*

EF: I don't know, because the boy is so totally into the television set. The viewer might make that projection. But maybe the fetish figure is letting the boy know what he doesn't consciously know— that the woman is undressing.

DK: *There are many discrepant elements in the work. Is that an important part of its sense?*

EF: Yes. The fetish figure is a kind of doll, and there are other dolls in the room. There are culturally normal elements. There is a doll that has no power at all. It just belongs in a girl's room.

DK: *You talk very psychologically about the scene, and about its interpersonal subtleties. Have you read much psychological literature?*

EF: No. I read a little of Jung. I've never read Freud, even though my work has been connected to his ideas. I understand his ideas have been discredited as too personalized. Nonetheless, he laid out the basic point of view. I think I am as primitive as he was, if not possessed of the same genius. My dramas do imply the primitive basic understanding of Freud's psychology.

DK: *Let's talk a little about the art business, to go from the sublimely to the ridiculously primitive. What do you think of your success? Does the high commodity value of your art affect the character of your production?*

EF: It would be a lie to deny that it has not had an influence on me, but I'm not sure of the nature of the influence. There's so much awe and wrongheaded thinking about success and fame. They certainly change your relationship with other artists. Our society in general wants stars, but it just as readily dismisses them. Cadillac dealers and chefs are stars. Everybody is a star. Plastic surgeons. Skin divers. It shows how thrilled we are with ourselves.

To me, success is clarity. The paintings become successful when they become clear. There is no greater success than when an audience can appreciate that clarity. The pressure to achieve clarity is the greatest pressure of all. The problem is that cultural enthusiasm moves faster than your ability to achieve clarity, and that gives you premature, false success. It grows out of proportion and prevents real success. Your media success moves faster than your artistic success. So you get used up real quick.

DK: *You've had a lot of attention.*

EF: Yes. That's a real, seductive pressure. If you get addicted to it, you start doing things to maintain the attention. You subtly change your progam of making art. I can't comment on the difficulty of making art after the success has passed, because that hasn't happened to me yet, but I live with the feeling that it is about to happen. It will occur. Then I will become less successful, disdained, ignored. It will happen within my lifetime and probably quickly. So I try to focus on my priorities, which I think are fairly good. I try to keep my instincts, which were fairly good from the start. The hardest thing for an artist to do, especially in New York, is to close the door of the studio to work—to shut the world out. You need time to concentrate and to focus. But the world gets in in funny ways. Obviously, it can come in through a telephone. It can come in through commissions. There are many things that are more interesting and fun to do than they are productive. They're more fun than making art because art is not fun. It's a drag. It's more fun to be photographed by famous photographers or to accept a titillating offer. It's more exciting to be interviewed by famous critics and to have books made about you. It's exciting to show in foreign countries because then you can visit them and don't have to be in your studio working. You can be social. It's very hard to shut the social out. You have to be very disciplined. You have to want the art you make to be taken more seriously than you are. You want the art to have a better life than you do. Today artists often get more attention than their art. The artist has all the fame. The objects don't get nearly enough attention. It's important to keep that in mind. To become more famous than your work is to reverse the order that you've established as a thing-maker. And artists are boring. Within the large context of society, they're pretty boring. As for the commodity question, I don't know whether it really makes a difference or not. I think that there's a degree of security in knowing that somebody who values money is willing to respect your work the way he respects money. It's depressing that only a very small percent of the population can afford to buy your work. If it's true that the work doesn't reach the larger population, then that has to change. That's particularly important for me, since I have tried to make my work go to the center of our social reality. I know I've succeeded when my work is talked about as though it were a movie that had just been seen. Writers have taken the characters in a very literal way.

DK: *You seem to want your art to be popular.*

EF: Yes, in the sense that I want it to name the way we understand ourselves.

DK: *What do you think about the critical response to your painting? Do you feel your work is understood?*

EF: I think so. The language of art criticism has changed to accommodate art's move into figuration, or more precisely into a kind of personal figuration. This is reflected in the number of poets who write criticism now, in contrast to the sixties and seventies, when philosophers took over.

DK: *You've mentioned guarding your time, being disciplined. What kinds of work habits to you have?*

EF: I try to work every day. I like to work between eleven and five or ten and six, like a daytime job. I find that I can concentrate for about four hours. I have to carve out this time, eleven to five, but I'll probably only work three or four hours in that period. I have to feel that I have the whole time to do it. I hate starting paintings. It is terrible to stand in front of a canvas, knowing that whatever you're first going to think about isn't what is going to be there ultimately. It just looks like work, a lot of work.

The first several days of painting are almost blindfolded. The first day I might just cover the canvas with color or some image. It's just to get rid of all that white, or to begin to get a surface. I'll knock stuff around in an absentminded or erratic way, not making any hard decisions, until I reach the point at which I've rendered something that I like. When I have, when I've found something that I really like, then I want to save it. This means that I have to make the rest of the painting come up to it. That's when the painting becomes concentrated and specific decisions are being made. Usually what happens is that the rest of the painting has moved beyond the part that I was trying to save. That part is holding the rest of the painting back. So I have to destroy the part that I loved. That's a very painful, frightening moment. I don't like people around when I'm doing that. I don't actually like people around at all when I paint. I develop my isolation. I do have an assistant, but she's here only in the morning. Sometimes her time and mine overlap, but basically I don't paint around her. When those moments of change occur, I feel very vulnerable. I feel I'm going into the unknown. I don't like to be watched when I'm doing that.

DK: Do you use preliminary sketches or photographs?

EF: I use photographs I've taken. I took a lot of photographs of figures on the beaches of Saint-Tropez. The people are naked and they're behaving in a social way. I can watch the social language of the naked body. I love the contradiction between the nakedness and the sociality. It's not like pornography, which is the other social place you can get photographs of naked bodies. Pornography is such a specific language. It's so confrontational and so limited to just what it is. In Saint-Tropez people are naked and you watch them being themselves. You know they could be making a telephone call. They'd be just naturally talking on the phone or cooking or whatever. It's a social language, so I use that, and I collage things together. One figure from one photograph, one from another. My backgrounds come from magazine photographs.

DK: *What does collage mean to you?*

EF: It's something that's always fascinated me because it's modernist yet it can be put to postmodernist use. Collage initially reflected the atomization of the world. It was about reconstructing the pieces to make a wholly new kind of experience, which nonetheless did not add up to a picture of the whole world, a new totalization of the world. It's an incredible invention. It's as important to creative awareness as perspective was when it was invented. Perspective gave you a mathematical equivalent of the way we see in space. Collage gives you a technique approximating the way we think. It's a conceptual, not a perceptual order.

I think the impetus for early modernism was to explode the historical and cultural world, and proceed from there. What I find I'm doing, in this late modernist period, is to reconstitute the whole culture from fragments. I use a collage technique, but to a different purpose. I think there is an integral whole, difficult as it is to articulate, not just a pile of fragments. I want a seamless look constituted by fragments.

DK: *There seems to be a convergence of photography and painting in your work.*

EF: Yes, but their roles are reversed now. Painting used to be the dominant mode, and photography was a new technology that imitated painting. Now photography is the dominant mode of representation and painting is trying to reclaim some of its territory, but from a diminished point of view.

DK: *But didn't you say that painting can give you a concentrated, poignant moment of meaning that photography isn't capable of?*

EF: Yes, that's my call to arms, my credo. That had better be true.

That is what I think is essentially the difference and that's why I'd rather paint than take photographs.

DK: *Photography seems to diffuse meaning.*

EF: That's an interesting idea. I recently saw a photograph by Rudy Burckhardt. It's one of his famous photographs of the Flatiron Building, a black-and-white photograph, from about 1949. It is the quintessential New York street scene. It's an urban landscape taken up high. It really captures the sense of place, showing it in a positive light—somehow it celebrates place. But you get the sense that in the next minute it's going to change. It won't stick. That's its cynicism. In the dominant type of photograph, the snapshot of people in action, you get an offhand look, a gesture caught at the right moment. It is always revealing, but it has a very cynical edge to it. It is very nonempathic, showing how disappointing or untidy human beings are. It's embarrassing and awkward in its lack of empathy.

DK: *Some people have said your work is cynical, unempathic. Is that the photographic aspect of it?*

EF: I think the charge is based on a misunderstanding. I work with an overexposed imagery that nonetheless remains taboo. I'm struggling to articulate the emotional meaning in such images. The cynicism is really the audience's, not mine. We've had too much visual stimulus in our society. We've seen too much imagery in too many different contexts. We no longer know the precise meaning of what we see. We are being overwhelmed, and so we become ironic and cynical in defense. We're living too much on a picture stage. I recognize that my work is part of that situation, but I am sincerely trying to discover meaning, to make the meaning of my images directly experienceable. I hope I'm not adding to the meaninglessness.

DK: *The art world has become international, no doubt adding to the glut. How do you feel, as an American artist, in the international context? Do you think of yourself as a specifically American artist, or in some way a more broadly based—"international"—artist?*

EF: I'm an American artist the way Baselitz and Kiefer are German artists. Clemente's an Italian artist and Bill Woodrow is an English sculptor. National identity is the international currency these days. It's ironic in the face of modernism's ambition, the ambition of the international style. But "international style" is now made up of national identities. I don't see this as a liability. It's the reason new attention has been focused on the Germans, even though they haven't made any artistic breakthroughs, certainly not any more than the Italians or Americans or whoever. There is a new privatism, which is inseparable from the new nationalism. There is a social and historical awareness of art. It seems very particular to a place and history. It's as though the domestic has become an instrument of artistic advance. The dramatic turmoil in domestic life is for me a metaphor for today's internationalism, as well as for the larger predicament of the meaning of the human in today's world.

The Germans caught our attention because they could turn to artistic advantage a dramatic historical event the way I try to turn to advantage my sense of the American adolescent as a debilitated person. In our different ways, we convey a tragic sense of the world, a search for self-identity by putting back the pieces artistically. You try to figure the meaning out artistically. The Germans point to the big historical event of their defeat in World War II as a way of dealing with profound emotions—guilt, anger, the loss of a sense of identity, all displaced into art. It is easier to respond to the art than to the reality—or to the reality filtered through the art, rather than to the reality directly. The art helps you know the emotional reality. I'm being very theatrical and simplistic, but the art works partly because an audience can readily identify with it, and the sense of art being related to social history helps the identification process. The horror of German history helps the feeling for the art. We Americans don't have the same thing on the same scale, but I, for one, want to deal with the kind of feelings aroused by such history. It's a way of coming to terms with who I am.

DK: *You seem to identify with the German artists in some way.*

EF: Well, I have consciously identified with Kiefer and Baselitz. They probably wouldn't agree with my analysis of their work, but I think I'm right. We're struggling for the same psychological end.

DK: *Have you shown much in Europe?*

EF: To an extent. There is definitely a feeling of chauvinism in Europe. It's very unfortunate, because it wrecks the spirit operating in all the art. However, the Europeans are more accepting of figuration. It was never really lost for them. In America, my work, which is stylistically not new, can appear new, because for a long time dramatic figuration was out.

DK: *About how many works do you make a year?*

EF: Between seven and ten pieces.

DK: *Large pieces?*

EF: Yes. I also do some smaller ones. I don't usually make studies for my work. I do little paintings on paper, sketches and things like that. But I don't do too many small canvases as studies.

DK: *You've mentioned that you traveled to Saint-Tropez. Do you go there regularly?*

EF: Yes.

DK: *Do you have other favorite spots?*

EF: Not really. I go to Arizona to visit my family, which is a favorite spot of sorts. There's a lot of stimulation there.

DK: You're very interested in the naked body. Do you have any thoughts about nakedness?

EF: Well, it still causes problems and anxieties, even after all its exposure in all kinds of ways. It still causes tremendous discomfort because it still seems like confrontation. Also, the forms of the body are much more interesting to paint than folds and cloth. I like flesh tones.

DK: Can one say that your naked bodies are deliberately not idealized?

EF: Yes. It may be puritanical, but I just can't bring myself to indulge in style and idealize anything. I'm a pragmatist and realist in that sense. Also, I think it is harder to empathize with an ideal. Idealization would undermine my sense of tragedy.

DK: Tragedy implies a sense of vulnerability. Does the naked body interest you because of its potentially tragic vulnerability?

EF: Yes. It's terrifically vulnerable, really exposed.

DK: Many of your naked bodies are ugly, as though you wanted to go to the opposite extreme from idealization. Is this deliberate on your part?

EF: I don't think they're deliberately ugly. If you look at the body, especially on the beach, you'd really be hard pressed to find a beautiful one, male or female. They're variations on a theme. I'm interested in the way a naked body can be made to reveal a social reality, and thus become disruptive for reasons other than its nakedness. I'm interested in the way the body can be coded to reveal what is socially unconscious yet omnipresent.

DK: You seem to want to use the naked body to be disruptive in a variety of ways.

EF: I want to be disruptive, but not as a revolutionary, nor just to throw a temper tantrum. I want to be disruptive simply to allow for the experiences that are dramatic to be taken dramatically.

DK: *It's been said that the eighties are the decade of content rather than form. Is your work more significant as content than form?*

EF: Perhaps. It sets up content in both a narrow sense and a broad sense. There's a very specific subject matter. But there's also the puzzle of its significance, which works through form. I present a situation in which people are forced to behave, but I don't know how they will, or what it will mean, as this comes through in the formal tensions.

You have to meditate on the possibilities. That's the moral dimension to the work. It's not just about a socially charged theme like incest or sexual initiation. You the viewer have to decide what your relationship to the theme is, and so you help create the possible outcome and meaning.

DK: *Is the content in the interpretation?*

EF: Exactly.

DK: *I have one last question. Your work has been called sexist. Is it?*

EF: The feminists have said I am, and they're wrong. The accusation comes from people who aren't looking at the paintings carefully. My show at the ICA in London was picketed by women against violence to women. They sent in a list of complaints about specific paintings. One of the paintings was *Master Bedroom*, which shows a young girl kneeling on a bed, stripped except for her underpants, her hair in rollers. She is hugging her dog. The light is coming in from the side, which implies an open door, an open bathroom door perhaps. And it implies another presence. She's looking in that direction. It implies a presence that is coming into or leaving the room. They said that I had set it up. Your first impression from a distance is that the girl has a smile on her face.

This supposedly means that she is pleasantly or playfully—perhaps erotically—anticipating the attention of whoever is coming in the door. The interesting thing about painting a smile is that when you paint it you freeze it, and a frozen smile turns into a grimace. The painting is painted in such a way that as you come from fifteen feet away to six feet away—as you move toward the painting—you realize that her look is a frozen grimace. This changes her relationship to whoever is coming in that door. The feminists assumed it was a man. I was trying to set up the situation of a victim. The feminists thought I was showing the old sexist idea that women who are raped entice their victimizer. That's her smile. But what looks like a welcoming grin turns into nightmarish anticipation. They didn't see that second reading, and thus they missed empathizing with the person in the picture. Also, I don't show her as a one-dimensional sexual object. Rather, I deal with the whole situation and her potential for nobility in it.

In the painting of the sisters, for example, which is the painting of the women in the bathroom, the striking thing is that you're in a private place. It's the only part of the house that you, as a male child, wouldn't be allowed into. It's your sisters' place, a completely private place. You definitely can't be in there. So it's a room with a double meaning to it, which is a compelling kind of situation to depict. The women in the picture are interesting because to me they're superficially alike but deeply opposite. I'm fascinated by their differentness.

One is definitely an athlete, an outward-looking, physical being. She's confident of herself. She's not self-consciously wiping herself on the bidet. She's rigorously and unself-consciously doing it. She's pure libido. The other woman is the alter ego. She's domesticated, checked, nurturing. With her voluptuous pear shape, she's classical. I just put them in the same room together. I don't see that as a statement against women at all. The main thing is their contrast, and that you're in this private room you shouldn't be in. It's positive in the sense that the women aren't doing anything wrong. I'm not criticizing them for being alone, for being intimate. The untitled painting of the two women, one on the bed, the other standing, is about how they're looking at you because you don't belong there. It's not that they're doing something wrong. They want you to reconsider your position. I'm not advocating evil; I'm talking about relationships.

DK: Well, I thought I had asked you the final question, but your last statement was so provocative in its response to the charge that your work was sexist, that I thought I would raise another sensational, troubling question—if one not strictly personal—in the hope of getting another provocative answer. We've already spoken about the commercial success of your art. Would you care to say anything about the increasing pre-occupation of the art world with money—the increasing connection between art and money, as though each needed the other in some peculiar way, apart from capitalism's ongoing search for ever more novel commodities? The recent auctions brought new highs for the works of many living artists. The Wall Street Journal *and* The New York Times *had front-page stories on the extraordinarily high prices being paid for art. It's been said that capitalism reduces every cultural product to its exchange value, washing the meaning out of it. Do you think this is true?*

EF: Well, I was always aware of the money issue, but I never paid special attention to it until recently. I also used to think, rather matter-of-factly and no doubt naïvely, that money was a positive influence, since it supported a lot of important activity. Now I am beginning to have some doubts. Money is a completely neutral form of exchange; for that reason it was a great invention. Money reduces every exchange to a common denominator. Art, on the other hand, is anything but a neutral form of exchange. It is quite the opposite. It is the giving of something you love to get something else you love. The problem I have and I think most people have is not really knowing how to turn money into something that is not money. A lot of collecting being done today is speculative, which means that collectors are turning their money into Art until it makes more money for them. And this is a big problem. The problem, as I see it, isn't wanting more of what you love; it's loving something neutral.

DK: *Do you think the preoccupation with money in the art world will affect the production of art itself?*

EF: I don't know. Probably. I recently saw a lithograph that Sarah Charlesworth was working on. It was a blowup of a plaid like you see in a 3M label. It is totally cynical. It is saying that nobody in the art-buying public—anywhere in this society—deserves better "art" than this. It is all the same to them. Art only means something on the crassest level, so give it to them.

DK: *What you seem to be saying is that today's young cynical artists have become like the cynical audience.*

EF: Exactly.

DK: *Is their work another "postmodern" demonstration of the convergence of avant-garde and kitsch in one art, carried to the point where they become indistinguishable? Kitsch is supposed to articulate the lowest common denominator stereotypes. Are today's cynics simply throwing the most common, stereotypical appearances of the society back in its face, the way Charlesworth is doing?*

EF: I think so. That's a good way of understanding their cynicism. However, while their work may be kitsch, it aims to be subversive and intolerable, to create change. I don't know that it will do that. What Sarah Charlesworth, Jeff Koons, Peter Halley, Sherrie Levine and others are saying, I think, is that there is no longer anything to give except objects you can't get anything from. At least, as David [Salle] has pointed out to me, he suffers from his ambivalence toward his cynicism, and it is this ambivalence which I think is the crucial element, because it admits to the desire for fulfillment and for pleasure at the risk of finding that it may not be possible.

DK: *Hasn't the idea of being subversive become a cliché in the art world?*

EF: Yes. Nonetheless, it underlies modernism, which assumes that art is always in a state of flux with respect to society—in ambivalent relationship to it—and wants to overthrow it, no doubt in some indeterminate way. But it's true that subversiveness may become a cliché, melodramatized; a lot of would-be subversive art today looks simply melodramatic, like Hollywood movies. Today, we've come to see modernism as a closed system, much like a game board, with rules and regulations. And it is as if at this time some players on the board have decided that making backward moves, or skipping spaces, or simply not moving at all are strategies as radical and subversive as moves by players that have gone before them. That's how deep our cynicism for modernism as some kind of tool for change has become.

I recently saw *The Color of Money*. It was a big film, with a good soundtrack and big actors and a good screenplay and good photography. But nothing came together; it was a pastiche of genre. For example, one of the most important scenes was when Paul Newman comes into the main exhibition pool hall at Atlantic City as if he were walking into a cathedral, and everything about that scene—the music, the way the camera panned down from the ceiling of this cavernous space onto the spectacle of the empty pool tables—was telling you, this is the big event, the main event. But it was a scene you'd seen played out a hundred times already. And Scorsese, rather than finding a way of reinventing that scene, merely called up all the hundred times you'd seen it. So all you could do was wait for it to be over, because you got it right away. This is typical of art today. Everything has a sensational scale to it, which attempts to disguise the fact that everything is overused and reused, including the idea of subversiveness.

This is a general problem: it's a problem of cliché and a feeling of collapse. It's something I saw in *Glengarry Glen Ross*, the Mamet play that was sort of a remake of *Death of a Salesman*. There's this sense of history being fragmented, having exploded, and there are these fragments lying on the ground that we're trying to pick up and put back together. It's a history of meaning, not a history of images, and yet the only thing we seem to be able to come up with is a history of images. I think you see this clearly in Julian's [Schnabel] work.

DK: *I see you want to live dangerously: you've critically introduced your contemporaries. Let's pursue your gambit. Within the context of the understanding you've set up, who are the artists you find interesting? Why do they make a difference within it?*

EF: Well, in the mid-seventies, when sincerity and/or meaning became important again, after pop art and minimalism and conceptual art, some artists found it either in direct expression of meaningfulness, or they found meaningfulness in the direct expression of meaninglessness, and that's how the lines were drawn. When I came to New York in the late seventies, the greatest risk was sincerity. The German artists—Kiefer, Baselitz, Polke, Lüpertz, Immendorff, Penck—became noteworthy because they were working with a historical event that was guaranteed to be meaningful. It was the worst thing that had happened, they were the descendants of its perpetrators, and they were trying to figure out who they were in relation to it. The whole struggle for meaning since the 1970s has been a struggle for identity. It's pervasive, but most of us can't identify what happened except in personal terms. By what happened, I mean what went wrong, what gave us this sense of collapse or disappointment. The Germans were hurt not just personally but culturally as well. It's very hard for us in America to complain or to feel that our complaint is justified, because, after all, what are we complaining about? That the objects we surround ourselves with are disappointing? I mean, it's a joke, we're more embarrassed about having believed in the superficial qualities of America, and it's hard to see yourself heroic in that light. But because the Germans were so devastated culturally, you can identify with their struggle for renewal. Baselitz made a formal decision to turn his images upside down. Before that he had been making traditional realist pictures, often genre and figure scenes. So he decided to turn history upside down. He distanced himself from history, almost as a kind of penitence, a kind of self-ostracism.

DK: He wouldn't agree with your interpretation. He'd say he was confirming the abstractness of his pictures.

EF: That's true. But abstract painting distances one from reality. By turning his paintings upside down, Baselitz was removing himself from cultural time in much the same way that some American Indian cultures would conduct purification rituals in which they would for a period of time reverse everything—their names, their behavior. Both Kiefer and Immendorff are dealing with their histories by reexamining their cultural figures and myths in a kind of holistic way, trying to see the good ones and the bad ones in some overall context. Immendorff's *Café Deutschland* is like a purgatory of modern-day Germany.

DK: What do you think of the Italian artists?

EF: For me, Clemente is the most interesting. I'm in awe of the psycho/sexual/religious quality of his work. He's so unafraid of his own erotic fantasies.

DK: Do we have to think of the more interesting new art in national terms?

EF: What has happened to the idea of an international style is that it has become an international language of national identities. Nationalism—the issue of national identity—can be used to deal with the collective international crisis of identity. The German situation in its way, and the Italian in its way, reflects a larger problem of the meaning of individual or personal identity in a world in which it seems meaningless—in a world whose scale denies its importance.

DK: Who are your favorite American artists?

EF: For me, David Salle is the smartest artist around. I find his work the most compelling. It seems frighteningly right. His work introduced me to the seriousness of our sense of meaninglessness. It created the most anxiety in me. I found it profoundly appalling. His pictures are very iconoclastic, the way they combine high art aspirations with his personal, autobiographical concerns. They are very bold in the way they throw him as well as high art out the window, in effect asserting that the problem of meaninglessness is insoluble. It is one thing to find culture meaningless, another, more courageous thing, to find one's own life meaningless—to find one's own desire for love, and the despair it generates, meaningless as well. Salle makes a high art out of meaninglessness.

I also like Malcolm Morley, who reminds me of Polke and Richter. He's anarchistic. He gives you a lot of sensuous surface to keep you interested, but he's really giving you nothing. His depiction is a destructive act of taking things apart, shredding them into nothing. For all the aggression with which he gets there, he leads to a very subtle kind of nothingness.

All the artists I find interesting raise the same core question: What is art? There is greater urgency than ever in this question. Modernism is based on it, but it has become a personal rather than simply an epistemological matter. It has become a matter of need. In the artists I've mentioned, the need for art has replaced the game of art, which the earlier questioning of art led to. Modernism asked "What is art?" in order to make subtle new art. Today, artists seriously ask "What is art?" not abstractly and provocatively, but because they have a need for art, and they want to know what it is they have a need for, and why. It is like having a need for a self, when it would be easier to get along without one.

DK: *You're implying that there's something pessimistic and personally— desperately—speculative in this.*

EF: That's true. I find Salle's art very pessimistic, and a kind of concrete speculation more about himself than about the abstract nature of art. Or rather, the two are inseparable for him. He tests the claim of credibility made by different kinds of past art and different kinds of present self.

DK: You seem to imply an irresolution in this widespread speculation.

EF: That's true.

DK: Do you think that the artist should accept assimilation gracefully because it's going to happen to him anyway?

EF: Well, assimilation is not exactly defeat. Personally speaking, being assimilated makes me feel integrated. I can get on with doing what I have to do. Artists don't want to be alone. Otherwise why would they bother making things that others could see?

UNTITLED SERIES

UNTITLED, 1986.
Charcoal/paper; 24″ × 18″.
Collection of Fredrik Roos, Sweden.
Courtesy Mary Boone Gallery.
Photo: Zindman/Fremont.

Untitled, 1986.
Charcoal/paper; 24″ × 18″.
Collection of Mr. and Mrs. Leo Castelli, New York.
Courtesy Mary Boone Gallery.
Photo: Zindman/Fremont.

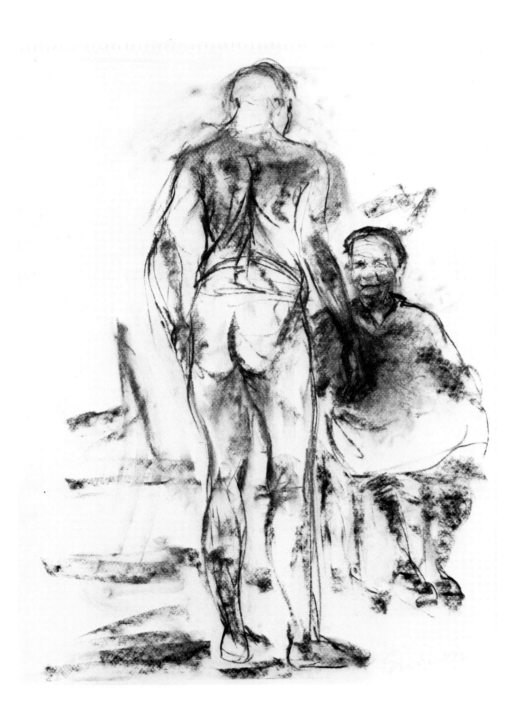

SOLO EXHIBITIONS

1975   Dalhousie Art Gallery, Halifax, Nova Scotia, Canada.

1976   Studio, Halifax, Nova Scotia, Canada.
       Galerie B., Montreal, Canada.

1978   Galerie B., Montreal, Canada.

1980   Edward Thorp Gallery, New York, New York.
       Davis Art Gallery, University of Akron, Akron, Ohio.

1981   Sable Castelli Gallery, Toronto, Canada.
       Edward Thorp Gallery, New York, New York.

1982   Edward Thorp Gallery, New York, New York.
       University of Colorado Art Galleries, Boulder, Colorado.
       Sable Castelli Gallery, Toronto, Canada.

1983   Sir George Williams Art Galleries, Montreal, Canada.
       Saidye Bronfman Centre, Montreal, Canada.
       Larry Gagosian Gallery, Los Angeles, California.
       Galleria Mario Diacono, Rome, Italy.
       Multiples Inc., New York, New York.

1984   Mary Boone Gallery, New York, New York.

1985   Mendel Art Gallery, Saskatoon, Canada.
       Van Abbemuseum, Eindhoven, The Netherlands.
       Kunsthalle Basel, Basel, Switzerland.

Institute of Contemporary Arts, London, England.
Art Gallery of Ontario, Toronto, Canada.
Sable Castelli Gallery, Toronto, Canada.
Mario Diacono Gallery, Boston, Massachusetts.

1986   Whitney Museum of American Art, New York,
            New York.
        Mary Boone Gallery, New York, New York.
        Larry Gagosian Gallery, Los Angeles, California.
        Daniel Weinberg Gallery, Los Angeles, California.
        University Art Museum, Long Beach, California.

1987   Mary Boone Gallery, New York, New York.

GROUP EXHIBITIONS

1975   "Canada Canvas," Time-Life of Canada. Traveling
        exhibit throughout Canada put together by Time-Life.

1976   "Seventeen Artists: A Protean View," Vancouver Art
        Gallery, Vancouver, British Columbia, Canada.

1978   "Neun Kanadisches Kunstlers," Kunsthalle Basel, Basel,
        Switzerland.
        Edward Thorp Gallery, New York, New York.
        Edward Thorp Gallery, New York, New York.

1981   "New York: Visiting Artists," Museum of Art, Rhode
        Island School of Design, Providence, Rhode Island.
        "Summer Pleasures," Barbara Gladstone Gallery, New
        York, New York.
        Edward Thorp Gallery, New York, New York.
        "Alumni Exhibition," California Institute of the Arts,
        Valencia, California.
        "The Reality of Perception," Robeson Center Gallery,
        Rutgers University, Newark, New Jersey.
        Edward Thorp Gallery, New York, New York.
        "Real Life Magazine," Nigel Greenwood Gallery, London,
        England.
        "Art for Your Collection," Museum of Art, Rhode Island
        School of Design, Providence, Rhode Island.
        "Large Format Drawings," Barbara Toll Fine Arts, New
        York, New York.

1982   "Narrative Settings," Josef Gallery, New York, New York.

"Critical Perspectives," Project Studio 1, Queens, New York.

1982 "By the Sea," Barbara Toll Fine Arts, New York, New York.
"Focus on the Figure: Twenty Years," Whitney Museum of American Art, New York, New York.
"The Expressionist Image: From Pollock to Today," Sidney Janis Gallery, New York, New York.
Edward Thorp Gallery, New York, New York.
"Figures of Mystery," Queens Museum, Queens, New York.
Milwaukee Museum, Milwaukee, Wisconsin.
"Drawing: An Exploration of Line," The Maryland Institute, College of Art, Baltimore, Maryland.

1983 "Reallegory," The Chrysler Museum, Norfolk, Virginia.
"Biennial," Whitney Museum of American Art, New York, New York.
"Group Drawing Exhibition," Daniel Weinberg Gallery, Los Angeles, California.
"Self Portraits," Linda Farris Gallery, Seattle, Washington.
"Mary Boone and Her Artists," Seibu Museum, Tokyo, Japan.
"Paintings," Mary Boone Gallery, New York, New York.
"Small Works," Bonnier Gallery, New York, New York.
"Back to the USA," Kunstmuseum Luzern, Luzern, Switzerland.
"Tendencias a Nueva York," Crystal Palace, Madrid, Spain.
"American Still Life," Contemporary Arts Museum, Houston, Texas.

1984 "Modern Expressionists," Sidney Janis Gallery, New York, New York.
"American Neo-Expressionists," The Aldrich Museum, Ridgefield, Connecticut.

1984 "New Painting," The Krannert Art Museum, Champaign, Illinois.

"Painting and Sculpture Today," Indianapolis Museum of Art, Indianapolis, Indiana.

"New Painting," Musée d'Art Contemporain, Montreal, Canada.

"An International Survey of Contemporary Painting and Sculpture," Museum of Modern Art, New York, New York.

"La Biennale di Venezia," Venice, Italy.

"Drawings," Mary Boone Gallery, New York, New York.

"The Human Condition: SFMMA Biennial III," San Francisco Museum of Modern Art, San Francisco, California.

"Aspekte Amerikanischer Kunst Der Gegenwart," Neue Galerie Sammlung Ludwig, Aachen, West Germany.

"Drawings after Photography," Allen Memorial Art Museum, Oberlin, Ohio.

"Large Drawings," Allen Memorial Art Museum, Oberlin, Ohio.

"Content," Hirshhorn Museum, Washington, D.C.

1985 Sable Castelli Gallery, Toronto, Canada.

"Biennial," Whitney Museum of American Art, New York, New York.

"XIIIᵉ Biennale de Paris," Paris, France.

"New Art '85," ARCA, Marseille, France.

Daniel Weinberg Gallery, Los Angeles, California.

"Carnegie International," Museum of Art, Carnegie Institute, Pittsburgh, Pennsylvania.

BIBLIOGRAPHY

Lehmann, Henry. "On Canvas From Sea to Sea." *Montreal Star,* January 1975.

Edinborough, A. "Time Counts the Years. . . ." *Financial Post,* January 18, 1975.

Greenwood, Michael. "Canada Canvas." *Artscanada,* March 1975, p. 3.

Chandler, John. "Seventeen Canadian Artists: A Protean View." *Artscanada,* October 1976.

Perrin, Peter. "Icon and Word." *Artscanada,* February 1978, pp. 44–47.

Bogardes, George. "Fischl Explores. . . ." *Montreal Star,* March 1978.

Van Jurg Kupper, Hans. "Metaphysik des Alltaglichen." *Baseler Zeitung,* June 11, 1978.

Bleckner, Ross. "Transcendent Anti-Fetishism." *Artforum,* March 1979, pp. 50–55. (Illus: *Family Scene,* p. 51, b&w.)

Rickey, Carrie. "Taste Test." *The Village Voice,* May 5, 1980, p. 83.

Pincus-Witten, Robert. "Entries: Palimpsest and Pentimenti." *Arts Magazine,* June 1980, pp. 128–131.

Zimmer, William. "Theme Song (and Dance)." *The Soho Weekly News,* June 2–8, 1980.

Touseley, Nancy. "Canadian Painting Aspects of the Seventies." *Vanguard,* Summer 1980, pp. 30–37.

Kelley, Patrick. "Eric Fischl: Paintings and Drawings." *Dialogue: The Ohio Arts Journal,* September/October 1980, pp. 46–48.

Anderson, Alexander, and Rickey, Carrie. "Up Against the Wall Street: An Investor's Guide to Galleries." *The Village Voice,* October 15, 1980.

Berlind, Robert. "Eric Fischl at Thorp." *Art in America,* November 1980, pp. 141–143. (Illus: *Sleepwalker,* p. 141, c.)

Staff. "Picasso: A Symposium." *Art in America,* December 1980, pp. 9–19.

J.M.B. "Eric Fischl Rages at Giants of Art." *The Globe and Mail,* February 14, 1981.

Staniszewski, Mary Anne. "Group Drawing Show." *Art News,* March 1981, p. 232.

Smith, Roberta. "Representation: An Abstract Issue." *The Village Voice,* March 11, 1981, p. 75.

de F. D. Smith, Valerie. "Group Show." *Flash Art,* March/April 1981, p. 42.

Lawson, Thomas. "Eric Fischl." *Artforum*, May 1981, pp. 70–72. (Illus: *Gals from the Office*, p. 72, b&w.)

Tatransky, Valentin. "Eric Fischl." *Arts Magazine*, May 1981, p. 34. (Illus: *After the Kill*, p. 34, b&w.)

Wylie, L. "Eric Fischl at Sable Castelli." *Artmagazine*, May 1981, p. 78.

Tatransky, Valentin. "Fischl, Lawson, Robinson and Zwack: They Make Pictures." *Arts Magazine*, June 1981, pp. 147–149. (Illus: *Help*, p. 148, b&w.)

Touseley, Nancy. "Eric Fischl at Sable Castelli." *Artscanada*, July/August 1981, p. 38. (Illus: *Last Resort*, p. 38, b&w.)

Pincus-Witten, Robert. "Entries: Snatch and Snatching." *Arts Magazine*, September 1981, pp. 88–91. (Illus: *Bad Boy*, p. 88, b&w; *First Sex*, p. 89, b&w; *Time for Bed*, p. 90, c; *Birth of Love*, p. 91, c.)

Lawson, Thomas. "Too Good to Be True." *Reallife*, Autumn 1981, pp. 3–6.

Fischl, Eric. "How I Make a Painting; Picture it. . . ." *New Observations 3*, October 5, 1981.

Owens, Craig. "Back to the Studio." *Art in America*, January 1982, pp. 99–107. (Illus: *Bad Boy*, p. 102, b&w.)

Mays, John Bentley. "Fischl Disturbs with Harrowing Oil." *The Globe and Mail*, January 30, 1982, p. 13 (entertainment section).

Schjeldahl, Peter. "Mind Over Matter." *The Village Voice*, March 9, 1982, p. 79.

Staff. "A Look at the Natural and Unnatural." *The Denver Post*, March 14, 1982, p. 11R.

Randolph, Jeanne. *Vanguard.* April 1982, p. 29.

Smith, Roberta. "Surface Values." *The Village Voice*, April 13, 1982, p. 80.

Diehl, Carol. "As Time Goes By." *Art and Auction*, May 1982, pp. 30–32.

Staff. *The Print Collector's Newsletter.* May/June 1982, pp. 56–58. (Illus: *Digging Kids*, p. 58, b&w.)

Friedman, Jon. "Reviews, Eric Fischl." *Arts Magazine*, June 1982, p. 21. (Illus: *The Women*, p. 21, b&w.)

Kuspit, Donald. "Reviews, New York." *Artforum*, Summer 1982, p. 85.

Ratcliff, Carter. "Contemporary American Art." *Flash Art*, Summer 1982, pp. 32–35. (Illus: *Bad Boy*, p. 33, c; *Digging Kids*, p. 34, b&w.)

Robbins, Corrine. "Ten Months of Rush-Hour Figuration." *Arts Magazine*, September 1982, pp. 100–103.

Bass, Ruth. "Reviews, Eric Fischl." *Art News*, September 1982, p. 176.

Becker, Robert. "Art: Creative Coupling." *Interview*, October 1982, pp. 82–85.

Mays, John Bentley. "Compelling Iconography Culled From Pain." *The Globe and Mail*, October 1982, p. 11 (entertainment section).

Smith, Roberta. "Every Man's Land." *The Village Voice*, October 26, 1982, p. 98.

Staff. "Eric Fischl at Sable Castelli." *Artscanada*, November 1982, p. 39. (Illus: *Day the Shah Ran By*, p. 39, b&w.)

Glueck, Grace. "The Artists' Artists." *Art News*, November 1982, p. 100. (Illus: *Grief*, p. 100, b&w.)

Ratcliff, Carter. "Expressionism Today: An Artists' Symposium." *Art in America*, December 1982, pp. 60–62, 69. (Illus: *Women*, p. 62, c.)

Webb, Marshall. "Eric Fischl at Sable Castelli." *Artmagazine*, December 1982–February 1983, pp. 39–40. (Illus: *Father and Son*, p. 39, b&w.)

Glueck, Grace. "Art: 'Figures of Mystery' Shows New York by 10." *The New York Times*, January 7, 1983, p. C20.

Preston, Malcolm. "Mystery in Queens." *Newsday*, January 7, 1983.

Chandler, Marcus. "Art World: Private Firm Challenges the Stereotypes of Art Collecting." *The Indianapolis Star*, February 6, 1983.

Schjeldahl, Peter. "Falling in Style." *Vanity Fair*, March 1983, pp. 115–116.

Yau, John. "How We Live: The Paintings of Robert Birmelin, Eric Fischl, and Ed Paschke." *Artforum*, April 1983, pp. 60–67. (Illus: *BB*, p. 61, c; *Beach Ball*, p. 64, b&w; *Catch*, p. 64, b&w; *Pizza Eater*, cover, c.)

Sabbath, Lawrence. "New York Artist Explores Social Taboos." *Montreal Gazette*, April 2, 1983, p. B7.

Toupin, Gilles. "Eric Fischl: Une Peinture du Malaise." *La Presse Montreal*, April 2, 1983, p. B22.

Staff. "Eric Fischl." *Kunstforum*, May 1983, pp. 56–59.

Kangas, Matthew. "Self Portraits: The Soul Observed." *Artsline*, August 1983.

Downey, Roger. "Linda Farris' 13th Anniversary Show: Self Portraits Without Self Revelation." *The Weekly*, August 3, 1983.

Glowen, Ron. "Heavyweight Artists Offer a Closer Look at Themselves." *Everett Herald*, August 5, 1983. (Illus: *Portrait with April*, b&w.)

Hackett, Regina. "47 Artists Picture Themselves, Some for Better, Some for Worse." *Seattle Post Intelligencer*, August 5, 1983.

Wallach, Amei. "The Parrish's Painterly Figures." *Newsday*, August 7, 1983.

Tarzan, Dennis. "Self Portraits." *The Seattle Times*, August 7, 1983, pp. E1–3.

Russell, John. "When Figure Paintings Capture the Energies of Life." *The New York Times*, August 7, 1983, Sec. 2/p. 21.

Johnson, Patricia C. "Still Life Show at CAM Spans Era of New Interest in Ancient Genre." *Houston Chronicle*, September 25, 1983, p. 14.

Kalil, Susie. "Painting: 'American Still Life 1945–1983.' " *The Houston Post*, September 25, 1983, p. F1.

Sturtevant, Alfred. "Out Takes from the American Dream." *Island*, October 1983. (Illus: *Dog Days*, b&w; *Bad Boy*, b&w; *Slumber Party*, b&w.)

Staff. "La Experiencia Neoyorkina." *Guia Del Ocio*, October 1983, art supplement, p. 107.

Logrono, Miguel. "Tendencias en Nueva York." *Diario*, October 1983, IV16.

M., S., "Las Tendencias Artisticas de Nueva York Irrumpen en Madrid." *ABC*, October 12, 1983, pp. 44–45.

Soler, Jaime. "New York, New York." *Diario,* October 12, 1983, p. 27.

Serraller, F. Calvo. "Los Bellos Ecos del Ultimo Grito Artistico." *El País,* October 15, 1983, pp. 1–2.

Guisasola, Felix. "La Academia del Nuevo ('Tendencias en Nueva York')." *Vardar,* November 1983, pp. 15–17.

Larson, Kay. "How Should Artists Be Educated?" *Art News,* November 1983, pp. 85–91

Staff. "Polemicas, 'Tendencias en Nueva York.' " *Guadalimar,* November 1983, pp. 6, 13–18.

Staff. "Nueva York." *El País,* November 1983, pp. 77–79.

Mays, John Bentley. "Close Encounters with Europe's 'New' Art." *The Globe and Mail,* November 5, 1983, p. E11.

Huici, Fernando. "El Día en que Nueva York Invadio Madrid." *El País,* November 6, 1983, p. 74.

Huici, Fernando. "Las Nuevas Tendencias de Nueva York se Exponen en el Retiro Madrileño." *El País,* November 6, 1983, p. 74.

Garcia, Angel Gonzalez. "Vanguardia Biologica." *Cambio 6,* November 7, 1983, pp. 141–145.

Willard, Marta. "El Sueño Americano." *Actual,* November 7, 1983, pp. 80–82.

Del Guercio, di Antonio. "Il Pupazzo e la Figura." *Rinascita,* November 18, 1983, p. 41.

Hume, Christopher. "Taking a Collection." *The Toronto Star,* November 19, 1983, p. F7.

Schloss, Edith. "Suzanne Santoro's Fiery Abstractions." *International Herald Tribune,* November 19–20, 1983.

O'Brien, John. "The Roman Art Scene." *Daily American,* November 20–21, 1983.

Schutz, Sabine. "Back to the USA." *Die Kunst,* December 1983, pp. 827–834. (Illus: *Untitled,* c.)

Robbins, Kevin. "Eric Fischl." *Upstart,* 1984, pp. 6–46. (Illus: *Cargo Cults,* p. 7, b&w.)

Linker, Kate. "Eric Fischl: Involuted Narratives." *Flash Art,* January 1984, pp. 56–58. (Illus: *Dog Days,* p. 56, c; *Birthday Boy,* p. 57, c; *Time for Bed,* p. 57, c; *Slumber Party,* p. 58, b&w.)

Ratcliff, Carter. "The Inscrutable Jasper Johns." *Vanity Fair,* February 1984, pp. 61–65.

Perry, Art. "Fischl Finds Obsessions in Suburbia." *Vancouver Province,* February 15, 1984, p. 43.

Kuspit, Donald. "Eric Fischl's America Inside Out." *C,* Winter 1984, pp. 14–17. (Illus: *Dog Days,* b&w; *A Visit to/A Visit from the Island,* b&w; *Sleepwalker,* b&w; *Slumber Party,* b&w.)

Panicelli, Ida. "Eric Fischl at Mario Diacono." *Artforum,* March 1984, p. 105. (Illus: *Birthday Boy,* p. 105, b&w.)

Ratcliff, Carter. "Spain: The Structure of the Ritual." *Vanity Fair*, March 1984, pp. 58–66.

Liebman, Lisa. "Eric Fischl's Year of the Drowned Dog." *Artforum*, March 1984, pp. 67–69.

Bass, Ruth. "New Editions: Eric Fischl." *Art News*, March 1984, pp. 82–83.

Hume, Christopher. "Fischl's Works Speak a Language That Everyone Can Understand." *Toronto Star*, March 10, 1984, p. M6.

Kelley, J. "American Art Since 1970: A Shaky Transition." *Artweek*, April 7, 1984, p. 1. (Illus: *A Visit to/A Visit from the Island*, p. 1, b&w.)

Schjeldahl, Peter. "Bad Boy of Brilliance." *Vanity Fair*, May 1984, pp. 67–72. (Illus: *Bad Boy*, p. 67, c; *Cargo Cults*, p. 68–69, c; *The Old Man's Boat and the Old Man's Dog*, p. 70, c.)

Staff. "Made in the USA, Ein Boser Realist." *Das Kunstmagazine*, May 1984, pp. 28–29.

Hullenkramer, Marie. "Magnet New York." *Art*, May 1984, pp. 28–29.

Atkins, Robert. "American Visions in Venice's Biennale." *Newsday*, May 6, 1984.

Sabbath, Lawrence. " 'Via New York' Attacks Cherished Beliefs, Styles." *Montreal Gazette*, May 12, 1984, p. A14.

Bourdon, David. "Paradise." *Vogue*, June 1984, p. 61.

Greenspan, Stewart. "A Funny Thing Happened on the Way to the Biennale." *Art and Auction*, June 1984, pp. 73–74.

Russell, John. "Art: Battered Venice Biennale Shows Will to Live." *The New York Times*, June 18, 1984, p. C14.

Shore, Joan Z. "The Biennale in Venice: A Mixed Bag Amid the Hoopla." *International Herald Tribune*, June 23–24, 1984.

Hughs, Robert. "Gliding Over a Dying Reef." *Time*, July 2, 1984. pp. 76–77.

Eliasoph, Phillip. "Museum Exhibit (sic) Shows Still Life Can Be Moving Art." *Southern Connecticut Newspapers Incorporated*, July 8, 1984, p. F1.

Bonetti, David. "Venice Biennale Confused, One-Sided." *The Boston Globe*, July 15, 1984.

Larson, Kay. "The Real Things." *New York Magazine*, July 16, 1984, pp. 58–59.

Glueck, Grace. "Art: American Still Life with the Accent on the Life." *The New York Times*, July 20, 1984, p. C21.

Glueck, Grace. "A Neo-Expressionist Survey That Is Worth a Journey." *The New York Times*, July 22, 1984, Sec. 2/pp. 25, 28.

Hoelterhoff, Manuela. "The Venice Biennale: No Paradise for Art." *The Wall Street Journal*, July 31, 1984.

Maecht, Adrien. "New York." *L'Art Vivant*, July/August 1984, p. 10. (Illus: *Time for Bed*, p. 10, b&w.)

Baker, Kenneth. "Eric Fischl: 'Year of the Drowned Dog.' " *The Print Collector's Newsletter*, July/August, pp. 81–84.

Kramer, Hilton. "MoMA Reopened: The Museum of Modern Art in the Postmodern Era." *The New Criterion*, Summer 1984, p. 41. (Illus: *Time for Bed*, p. 38, b&w.)

Kohn, Michael. "MoMA: An International Survey." *Flash Art*, Summer 1984, pp. 62–63.

O'Brien, Glenn. "Beat." *Interview*, September 1984, p. 206. (Illus: *Inside Out*, p. 206, c.)

Brenson, Michael. "The Menu Is Diverse and the Flavor Is Truly International." *The New York Times*, September 9, 1984, p. 39.

Newhall, Edith. "Galleries." *New York Magazine*, September 17, 1984, p. 68. (Illus: *The Brat II*, p. 66, c.)

Millet, Catherine. "A Propos de Quelques Artistes Americains." *Art Press*, October 1984, pp. 4–12.

Gibson, Eric. "American Still Life." *The New Criterion*, October 1984, pp. 70–75.

Boettger, Suzaan. "The Human Condition: Biennale III, San Francisco Museum of Modern Art." *Artforum*, October 1984, pp. 96–97.

Glueck, Grace. "Eric Fischl." *The New York Times*, October 12, 1984, p. C24.

Hagenberg, Roland. "Water Sports." *New York Talk*, October 12, 1984, p. 32–33. (Illus: *Sleepwalker*, b&w; *Cargo Cults*, b&w.)

Indiana, Gary. "The 'Private' Collector." *The Village Voice*, October 23, 1984, pp. 79–81, 85.

Smith, Roberta. "Eric Fischl." *The Village Voice*, October 30, 1984, p. 108.

Jensen, Kristian. "Amerikanak Kunst fra New York i Dag." *Kunstavisen*, October 30, 1984, p. 12.

Hagenberg, Roland. "Interview mit Eric Fischl in New York." *Berliner Kunstblatt*, October–December 1984, pp. 44–45.

Storr, Robert. "Desperate Pleasures." *Art in America*, November 1984, pp. 124–130. (Illus: *The Old Man's Boat and the Old Man's Dog*, cover, c; *Noon Watch*, p. 125, c; *A Visit to/A Visit from the Island*, pp. 126–127, c; *Bad Boy*, p. 128, b&w; *Sleepwalker*, p. 128, b&w; *St. Tropez*, p. 129, c; *Best Western*, p. 131, c.)

Stevens, Mark. "How to Make a Splash." *Newsweek*, November 5, 1984, pp. 85–86. (Illus: *Vanity*, p. 85, c.)

Yau, John. "Eric Fischl." *Artforum*, February 1985, pp. 85–86. (Illus: *Vanity*, p. 85, b&w.)

Pincus-Witten, Robert. "Entries: Analytical Pubism." *Arts Magazine*, February 1985, pp. 85–86. (Illus: *Sisters*, p. 85, b&w; *Daddy's Girl*, p. 86, b&w.)

Enright, Robert. "Eric Fischl." *Canadian Art*, Spring 1985, pp. 70–75. (Illus: *Best Western*, p. 71, c; *Daddy's Girl*, p. 72, c.)

Storr, Robert. "Eric Fischl ou les Plaisirs Désenchantes." *Art Press*, March 1985, pp. 42–45. (Illus: *Slumber Party*, p. 44, b&w.)

Holm, Stellen. "Eric Fischl." *Clic,* No. 3: March 1985, pp. 36–38. (Illus: *Bad Boy,* p. 38, b&w.)

Russell, John. "Whitney Presents Its Biennial Exhibition." *The New York Times,* March 22, 1985, p. 52.

Raynor, Vivien. "Art: Paintings at French Gallery Reflect City Life." *The New York Times,* March 31, 1985, p. 52.

Smith, Roberta. "Endless Meaning at the Hirshhorn." *Artforum,* April 1985, pp. 81–85.

Borsa, Joan. "Eric Fischl: Representations of Culture and Sexuality." *Vanguard,* April 1985, pp. 20–23.

Larson, Kay. "The Bad News Bearers." *New York Magazine,* April 8, 1985, pp. 72–73.

Tilroe, Anna. "Fischl Keert Vuilnisbak met Untieme Leven om." *De Volkskrant,* April 19, 1985, p. 11.

Lamoree, Jhim. "Drama's uit het Familie-Album." *Haagse Post,* April 20, 1985, pp. 48–49.

Godfrey, Stephen. "Fischl Exhibit Raises Eyebrows." *The Globe and Mail,* April 25, 1985, p. 17.

Venant, Elizabeth. "Rebel Expressions." *Los Angeles Times,* April 28, 1985, Calender pp. 4–7. (Illus: *A Brief History of North Africa,* cover, c.)

Honnef, Klaus. "Nouvelle Biennale de Paris." *Kunstforum,* May–June 1985, pp. 216–232. (Illus: *Vanity,* p. 218, c.)

Kulenkampff, Verena. "Chronist Alltaglicher Schrecken." *Art,* June 1985, pp. 56–65. (Illus: *A Brief History of North Africa,* pp. 56–57, c; *Cargo Cults,* pp. 60–61, c; *Best Western,* p. 62, c; *Inside Out,* p. 63, c; *The Power of Rock and Roll,* p. 64, c.)

Hughes, Robert. "Careerism and Hype Amidst the Image Haze." *Time,* June 17, 1985, pp. 78–83. (Illus: *Haircut,* p. 78, c.)

Larson, Kay. "Boomtown Hype—and Real Quality." *New York Magazine,* June 17, 1985, pp. 46–47. (Illus: *Portrait of the Artist as an Old Man,* p. 59, c.)

Perrone, Jeff. "The Salon of 1985." *Arts Magazine,* Summer 1985, pp. 70–73.

Liebmann, Lisa. "At the Whitney Biennial: Almost Home." *Artforum,* Summer 1985, pp. 56–61. (Illus: *Portrait of the Artist as an Old Man,* p. 59, c.)

Marzorati, Gerald. "I Will Not Think Bad Thoughts—An Interview with Eric Fischl." *Parkett,* No. 5: 1985, pp. 9–30. (Illus: *A Brief History of North Africa,* p. 11, c; *Cargo Cults,* p. 17, c; *Bad Boy,* p. 20, c; *Time for Bed,* p. 21, b&w; *Untitled,* p. 27, c; *The Old Man's Boat and the Old Man's Dog,* p. 29, c.)

Schjeldahl, Peter. "Post-Innocence, Eric Fischl and the Social Fate of American Painting." *Parkett,* No. 5: 1985, pp. 31–45. (Illus: *Birthday Boy,* p. 35, b&w; *Best Western,* p. 33, c; *Vanity,* p. 37, b&w; *Daddy's Girl,* p. 41, c.)

Curiger, Bice. "Eric Fischl." *Artscribe*, July–August 1985, pp. 24–28. (Illus: *Sisters*, p. 25, b&w; *The New House*, p. 26, b&w; *The Visit II*, p. 27, b&w; *The Last Resort*, p. 28, b&w.)

Pohlen, Annelie. "Eric Fischl, Kunsthalle Basel." *Kunstforum*, July–September 1985, pp. 288–289. (Illus: *Sleepwalker*, p. 288, c; *Father and Son Sleeping*, p. 289, c; *The Old Man's Boat and the Old Man's Dog*, p. 289, c; *Untitled*, p. 289, c.)

Rose, Barbara. "Fischl." *Vogue*, November 1985, pp. 402–405, 462. (Illus: *The Sheer Weight of History*, p. 403, c; *Savior Mother, Save Your Love(r)*, p. 404, c.)

Bohm-Duchen, Monica. "Eric Fischl, ICA London." *Flash Art*, October/November 1985, pp. 56–57. (Illus: *Master Bedroom*, p. 56, b&w.)

Berman, Avis. "Artist's Dialogue: Eric Fischl, Trouble in Paradise." *Architectural Digest*, December 1985, pp. 72–79. (Illus: *The Power of Rock and Roll*, p. 72, c; *Salad Days*, p. 76, c; *Mother and Daughter*, p. 76, c; *Saigon Minnesota*, p. 76, c.)

Fischl, Eric. "Figures and Fiction." *Aperture*, Winter 1985, pp. 56–59. (Illus: *Floating Islands*, p. 57, c; *Cargo Cults*, p. 59, c.)

Brenson, Michael. "Is Neo-Expressionism an Idea Whose Time Has Passed?" *The New York Times*, January 5, 1986, Sec. 2/pp. 1, 12. (Illus: *Best Western*, p. 1, b&w.)

Flam, Jack. "Staring at Fischl." *The Wall Street Journal*, January 6, 1986, p. 18.

Auer, James. "Fischl's Art Probes and Pains beneath Our Modern Masks." *Milwaukee Journal*, January 5, 1986, p. 8. (Illus: *Time for Bed*, p. 8, b&w.)

Russell, John. "Art: At the Whitney, 28 Eric Fischl Paintings." *The New York Times*, February 21, 1986, p. C25. (Illus: *Master Bedroom*, p. C25, b&w.)

McGill, Douglas. "Probing Society's Taboos—On Canvas." *The New York Times*, March 2, 1986, Sec. 2/pp. 1, 12.

Larson, Kay. "The Naked Edge." *New York Magazine*, March 10, 1986, pp. 58–59. (Illus: *Savior Mother, Save Your Love(r)*, p. 58, c.)

Staff. "Album: Eric Fischl." *Arts Magazine*, March 1986, pp. 114–115. (Illus: *Vanity*, p. 114, b&w; *A Brief History of North Africa*, p. 114, b&w; *Bad Boy*, p. 115, b&w; *Time for Bed*, p. 115, b&w.)

Kass, Ray. "Current Milestones." *Dialogue*, March/April 1986, pp. 17–19.

Schjeldahl, Peter. "Eric Fischl's Vanity." *Art and Text*, February–April 1986, pp. 56–58. (Illus: *Vanity*, p. 56, b&w.)

Indiana, Gary. "Peeping Tom." *The Village Voice*, March 18, 1986, p. 85. (Illus: *Saigon Minnesota*, p. 85, b&w.)

Russell, John. "Eric Fischl." *The New York Times*, March 14, 1986, p. C26.

McNeish, Amy. "Lust in Suburbia." *House and Garden*, April 1986, p. 44. (Illus: *Saigon Minnesota*, p. 44, c.)

Larson, Kay. "Basement Bargains." *New York Magazine*, April 7, 1986, p. 74.

Laurence, Michael. "Eric Fischl." *The West Hollywood Paper*, April 17, 1986, pp. 1–2. (Illus: *Manhattoes*, p. 2, b&w.)

Muchnic, Suzanne. "The Art Galleries, La Cienega Area." *Los Angeles Times*, April 18, 1986, p. 12. (Illus: *Fort Worth*, p. 12, b&w.)

Wilson, William. "Eric Fischl's Mock Taboos of Daily Life." *Los Angeles Times*, April 27, 1986, pp. 1–2. (Illus: *Master Bedroom*, p. 1, b&w.)

Berlind, Robert. "Eric Fischl at the Whitney and Mary Boone." *Art in America*, May 1986, p. 153. (Illus: *Manhattoes*, p. 153, c.)

Tomkins, Calvin. "The Art World, Real and Unreal." *The New Yorker*, May 12, 1986, pp. 99–101.

Perl, Jed. "Storytellers." *The New Criterion*, May 1986, pp. 57–63.

Salvioni, Daniela. "Eric Fischl: Mary Boone and the Whitney Museum." *Flash Art*, May/June 1986, pp. 54–55. (Illus: *Pretty Ladies*, p. 54, b&w.)

Bailey, David. "Men to Look at . . . Men to Watch." *Vogue*, June 1986, p. 251.

Danto, Arthur C. "Art: Eric Fischl." *The Nation*, May 31, 1986, pp. 769–772.

Kuspit, Donald. "Eric Fischl: Whitney Museum of American Art, Mary Boone Gallery." *Artforum*, Summer 1986, pp. 124–125. (Illus: *Saigon Minnesota*, p. 125, b&w.)

Staff. "Eric Fischl." *Current Biography*, June 1986, pp. 13–16.

Heartney, Eleanor. "Eric Fischl, Whitney Museum/Mary Boone." *Art News*, Summer 1986, pp. 141–142. (Illus: *Bayonne*, p. 142, b&w.)

Welish, Marjorie. "Contesting Leisure: Alex Katz and Erich Fischl." *Artscribe*, June/July 1986, pp. 45–47. (Illus: *Barbeque*, p. 1, c; *The Old Man's Boat and the Old Man's Dog*, p. 45. c; *A Brief History of North Africa*, p. 47, c.)

Howell, John. "Hot Artists, Suburban Muse." *Elle*, September 1986, pp. 294–296. (Illus: *Best Western*, p. 294, c.)

Grimes, Nancy. "Eric Fischl's Naked Truths." *Art News*, September 1986, pp. 70–78. (Illus: *A Brief History of North Africa*, pp. 70–71, c; *Sleepwalker*, p. 72, c; *A Woman Possessed*, p. 72, c; *Bad Boy*, p. 74, c; *Funeral*, p. 74, c; *Barbeque*, p. 76, c; *The Old Man's Boat and the Old Man's Dog*, p. 77, c; *Bayonne*, p. 78, c.)

DONALD KUSPIT

A 1983 winner of the prestigious Frank Jewett Mather Award for Distinction in Art Criticism given by the College Art Association, Donald Kuspit is a contributing editor at *Art in America* and a regular contributor to *Artforum*. He is also the editor of *Art Criticism* and writes for *Artscribe* (London), *Art Presse* (Paris), *C Magazine* (Toronto) and *Wolkenkratzer* (Frankfurt), among other magazines. He holds doctorates in philosophy from the University of Frankfurt and in art history from the University of Michigan and is a professor of art history and philosophy at the State University of New York at Stony Brook. He has written over five hundred articles, exhibition reviews and catalogue essays. His most recent book is *Leon Golub: Existentialist/Activist/Painter*. He has also written *The Philosophical Life of the Senses; Clement Greenberg, Art Critic* and *The Critic Is Artist: The Intentionality of Art*. He is a consultant for UMI Research Press, for which he has edited a series on contemporary American art critics, art theory and contemporary art.

Other books in

ELIZABETH AVEDON EDITIONS

VINTAGE CONTEMPORARY ARTISTS SERIES

FRANCESCO CLEMENTE

interviewed by Rainer Crone
and Georgia Marsh

ROBERT RAUSCHENBERG

interviewed by Barbara Rose

DAVID SALLE

interviewed by Peter Schjeldahl